ROYAL COURT

The Royal Court Theatre an⸺ ⸺ Gate Theatre Dublin present

SHINING CITY

by **Conor McPherson**

First performance at the Royal Court Jerwood Theatre Downstairs
Sloane Square, London on 4 June 2004.
First performance at the Gate Theatre Dublin on 23 September 2004.

London run supported by the ROYAL COURT PRODUCTION SYNDICATE

SHINING CITY

written and directed by **Conor McPherson**

Cast in order of appearance
Ian **Michael McElhatton**
John **Stanley Townsend**
Laurence **Tom Jordan Murphy**
Neasa **Kathy Kiera Clarke**

Designer **Rae Smith**
Lighting Designer **Mark Henderson**
Sound Designer **Ian Dickinson**
Casting **Lisa Makin**
Production Manager **Paul Handley**
Stage Managers **Rebecca Austin, Laura Routledge**
Costume Supervisor **Iona Kenrick**
Company Voice Work **Patsy Rodenburg**
Set built by **Marvellous Engineering**

The Royal Court and Gate Theatre Dublin would like to thank the following for their help with this production: Michelle Fairleigh, Will Fricker, Jason Isaacs, Aaron Marsden, Paul McCarthy, Peter McDonald, Ian Rickson.

THE COMPANY

Conor McPherson (writer and director)
For the Royal Court: Dublin Carol, The Weir (&
West End/Broadway).
Theatre includes: This Lime Tree Bower, St Nicholas
(Bush); The Good Thief, Rum and Vodka (Fly by
Night Theatre Company, Dublin); Port Authority
(Gate Theatre Dublin/New Ambassadors).
As director: Eden (Peacock/Abbey & West End).
Radio includes: This Lime Tree Bower, The Weir.
Film includes: I Went Down, Saltwater, The Actors,
Endgame.

Ian Dickinson (sound designer)
For the Royal Court: Lucky Dog, Blest Be the Tie,
Ladybird, Notes on Falling Leaves, Loyal Women, The
Sugar Syndrome, Blood, Playing the Victim, Fallout,
Flesh Wound, Hitchcock Blonde (& Lyric), Black
Milk, Crazyblackmuthafuckin'self, Caryl Churchill
Shorts, Imprint, Mother Teresa is Dead, Push Up,
Workers Writes, Fucking Games, Herons, Cutting
Through the Carnival.
Other theatre includes: Port (Royal Exchange,
Manchester); Night of the Soul (RSC Barbican); Eyes
of the Kappa (Gate); Crime & Punishment in
Dalston (Arcola Theatre); Search & Destroy (New
End, Hampstead); Phaedra, Three Sisters, The
Shaughraun, Writer's Cramp (Royal Lyceum,
Edinburgh); The Whore's Dream (RSC Fringe,
Edinburgh); As You Like It, An Experienced Woman
Gives Advice, Present Laughter, The Philadelphia
Story, Wolks World, Poor Superman, Martin
Yesterday, Fast Food, Coyote Ugly, Prizenight (Royal
Exchange, Manchester).
Ian is Head of Sound at the Royal Court.

Mark Henderson (lighting designer)
West End theatre includes: Tonight's The Night,
Arsenic & Old Lace, Our House, On an Average
Day, Up for Grabs, Chitty Chitty Bang Bang, Three
Sisters, A Midsummer Night's Dream, Amy's View,
The Iceman Cometh, The Judas Kiss, Grease, West
Side Story, Spend Spend Spend, Neville's Island,
Follies, Gasping, Carmen Jones, Mutiny, Copenhagen,
Indian Ink, Passion, A Saint She Ain't, The Distance
From Here, King Lear, Platonov, Faith Healer, The
Shape of Things, Lulu, Phedre, Britannicus, Naked,
Vassa, Plenty, Bash, Coriolanus (& Gainsborough
Studios), Richard II (& Gainsborough Studios);
Hamlet (& Broadway).
Other theatre includes: The Real Thing, Suddenly
Last Summer, Enter the Guardsman, Design for
Living (Donmar); Playboy of the Western World,
Racing Demon, Les Parent Terribles, Hamlet,
Murmuring Judges, The Absence of War, A Little
Night Music, Le Grande Magia, Antony & Cleopatra,
The Oedipus Plays (RNT); Cat on a Hot Tin Roof
(RNT/Broadway); The General from America, Kiss
Me Kate, Macbeth, The Family Reunion, The Lion the

Witch & the Wardrobe (RSC); Sunset Boulevard
(tour), Closer to Heaven (Really Useful Group).
Opera includes: ENO, The Royal Opera, WNO,
Opera North, Glyndebourne, Scottish Opera, Opera
De Nancy, Hong Kong Festival.
Dance includes: LCDT, Rambert, the Royal Ballet,
Scottish Ballet, Northern Ballet, SWRB.
Comedy includes: Eddie Izzard Sexie World Tour
2003, Victoria Wood 2001 Tour, Bottom 2001 Tour,
The League of Gentlemen, French & Saunders, Ruby
Wax Stressed Tour, Steve Coogan The Man Who
Thinks He's It, Eddie Izzard Definite Article, Rowan
Atkinson in Revue.
Television and film includes: Rowan Atkinson in
Boston, The Tall Guy, Under Milk Wood.
Awards include: Olivier Award for Best Lighting
(1992, 1994, 2001 & 2002).
Mark is an Associate Director of the RNT.

Tom Jordan Murphy
For the Royal Court: Blasted, The Beauty Queen of
Leenane (& Broadway).
Theatre includes: Henry IV, Sour Grapes (Peacock);
Lovely Betty, Behan Himself, Car Show 3, Charlotte'
Web (Corn Exchange); The Lonesome West (Druid)
A Life (Abbey); Troilus & Cressida (Oxford Stage
Company); Handbag (Actors Touring Company); True
Lines (Bush); Borstal Boy, Juno & the Paycock
(Gaiety); Snow (Bickerstaffe); Streets of Dublin, The
Hostage (Tivoli); 44 Sycamore (Red Kettle); Upstart
(Riverbank); Paint it White (Bewleys).
Film includes: Man About Dog, Intermission,
Benedict Arnold, Mystics, The Abduction Club,
Boxed, The General, Michael Collins, Adam & Paul,
In America.
Television includes: The Bill, Fair City.
Awards include: Tony Award in a Featured Role &
Theatre World Award (The Beauty Queen of
Leenane).

Kathy Kiera Clarke
Theatre includes: Scenes From the Big Picture
(RNT); Macbeth (Lyric, Belfast); Coronation Voyage,
Low Level Panic, Brilliant Traces (Prime Cut
Productions); Medea, Summit Conference, Damaged
Goods, Riders to the Sea, Jekyll & Hyde (Citizens
Theatre, Glasgow); Borders of Paradise (Palace
Theatre, Watford); Torquato Tasso (Lyceum,
Edinburgh); Factory Girls, Once a Catholic
(Tricycle).
Television includes: Silent Witness, Omagh, Pulling
Moves, Last Legs, Take a Girl Like You, Eskimo Day,
Chandler & Co, Head Over Heels, The Grass Arena
Flash McVeigh.
Film includes: Solid Air, Bloody Sunday, The Most
Fertile Man in Ireland, Mad About Harry, Hard Nut:
A Love Story, Omagh.

Michael McElhatton

Theatre includes: The Wexford Trilogy (Tricycle); An Ideal Husband (Gate Theatre Dublin); The White Devil (Project at The Mint); Car Show (Corn Exchange); Twenty Grand (Abbey, Dublin); Greatest Hits, The Way of the World (Project Arts Centre); A Decision Pure and Simple (Riverside); An Enemy of the People (Young Vic/West End); As You Like It (Rose Theatre); Midnight Court (Project Theatre); Wind in the Willows (Sheffield Crucible); Little Malcolm & His Struggle Against the Eunuchs (BAC/Basingstoke); Water Music (Cockpit Theatre).

Television includes: Vicious Circle, Rebel Heart, The Ambassador II, Helena, The Loser, Fergus's Wedding, Paths to Freedom.

Film includes: Spin the Bottle, Intermission, The Actors, Blow Dry, Saltwater, Crushproof, I Went Down.

Writing includes: Paths to Freedom, Fergus's Wedding, Spin the Bottle.

Rae Smith (designer)

For the Royal Court: Crazyblackmuthafuckin'self, Presence, Dublin Carol, The Weir (West End/Broadway/national & international tours); Some Voices, Trust.

Other theatre includes: Oliver Twist, The Servant, Cause Célèbre, Sarasine, Mrs Warren's Profession, The Letter (Lyric, Hammersmith); The Prince of Homburg (RSC/Lyric); Cymberline, Mysteria, Henry VI part 3 (RSC); A Midsummer Night's Dream, Port, Sherlock Holmes in Trouble (Royal Exchange, Manchester); Endgame, Juno & the Paycock (Donmar/Gramercy, New York); The Cocktail Party (Lyceum, Edinburgh); Closing Time (RNT); The Visit, Street of Crocodiles (RNT/Theatre de Complicite), Gormenghast (David Glass Ensemble).

Opera includes: The Magic Flute (Scottish Opera); Don Giovanni (Welsh National Opera); Turn of the Screw (Brighton Festival); The Maids (Lyric, Hammersmith).

Future works include: A Midsummer Night's Dream (La Monnaie, Brussels); The Ring Cycle (Strasbourg Opera House).

www.rae-smith.co.uk

Stanley Townsend

For the Royal Court: Under the Blue Sky.

Other theatre includes: Remember This, Guys & Dolls, The Little Clay Cart (RNT); The Weir (Duke of York's/Australian tour); The Gingerbread Mix Up (Andrews Lane, Dublin); Amphibians (Dublin Festival); The Wake, Trinity For Two, Sacred Mysteries (Abbey, Dublin); Art (Wyndhams Theatre); Prayers of Sherkin (Old Vic); Who Shall Be Happy? (Mad Cow Prod Tours); Pride & Prejudice, Oleanna, The Dream, The Double Dealer, The Cherry Orchard (Gate Theatre Dublin); Democracy (Bush); Speed-the-Plow (Project Arts); Someone to Watch Over Me (West Yorkshire Playhouse); The Plough & the Stars (Young Vic); Saint Oscar (Field Day); Sexual Perversity in Chicago, The Caucasian Chalk Circle, The Country Wife, Nightshade, The White Devil (Rough Magic); I Can't Get Started (Dublin/ Edinburgh Festival).

Television includes: Omagh Bombing, The Brief, Murder Squad, Fallen, Wire in the Blood, The Commander, Seventh Stream, Menace, Heartbeat, Station Jim, Table 12, Casualty, Best of Both Worlds, Active Defence, DDU, Ballykissangel, Peak Practice, Jonathan Creek, A Touch of Frost, Career Opportunities, Bliss, The Governor, The Bill, Parnell, Nighthawks, Fortycoats, Lost Belongings, Lapsed Catholics, Glenroe.

Film includes: Inside I'm Dancing, Tulse Luper II, Suzie Gold, Wondrous Oblivion, American Girl, Monsieur N, Mystics, The Van, My Friend Joe, Moll Flanders, Jake's Progress, Beyond Reason, Good Girls, In the Name of the Father, Blue Ice, Into the West, The Miracle, Taffin.

Stanley is a founding member of Rough Magic Theatre Company.

GATE THEATRE DUBLIN

The Gate Theatre has been, both artistically and architecturally, a landmark building in Dublin for over two hundred years. It was established as a theatre in 1928 by Hilton Edwards and Micheál MacLiammóir. Under their guidance, the Gate offered Dublin audiences a first introduction to the world of European and American avant-garde theatre, as well as vibrant productions from the modern and classic Irish repertoire. It was at the Gate that such luminaries as Orson Welles and James Mason began their prodigious acting careers. Today the theatre continues to attract the finest of creative talent and offers a stimulating and inclusive programme, appealing to theatregoers of all generations and from a broad spectrum of the population. The theatre is unique in that it has had only two artistic directorates in 75 years.

In December 1983 Michael Colgan became director of the Gate Theatre. Since then the Gate has continued to flourish, combining high quality productions with groundbreaking theatrical events. In 1991 the Gate became the first theatre in the world to present a full retrospective of the 19 stage plays of Samuel Beckett. This festival was repeated at the Barbican Centre in London and New York's Lincoln Center. The Gate produced two Pinter festivals in Dublin in 1994 and 1997 and produced four plays for the Harold Pinter Festival at Lincoln Center Festival, New York in 2001, of which The Homecoming opened in Dublin in June of that year. One for the Road and The Homecoming also toured to London.

The Gate has established unique relationships with renowned playwrights such as Samuel Beckett, Brian Friel, Frank McGuinness, Conor McPherson and Harold Pinter. Various productions over the years include the full canon of Oscar Wilde's work; Three Sisters starring Sinead, Sorcha and Niamh Cusack; A Streetcar Named Desire starring Frances McDormand; Molly Sweeney, directed by Brian Friel, which enjoyed an extensive run in New York; Juno and the Paycock, which played on Broadway as well as touring to Jerusalem and Edinburgh; and Waiting for Godot, which toured to Beijing and Shanghai as part of the Ireland China Festival in May 2004.

The Gate Theatre is a not-for-profit organisation administered by the Edwards-MacLiammóir Trust and funded in part by the Irish Arts Council.

SHINING CITY

written and directed by
Conor McPherson

From 23 September 2004
press night 28 September 2004

Gate Theatre Dublin

BOX OFFICE
+353 1 874 4045/874 6042
www.gate-theatre.ie

The Gate Theatre is grateful to the Irish Arts Council for its continued support.

THE ENGLISH STAGE COMPANY AT THE ROYAL COURT

The English Stage Company at the Royal Court opened in 1956 as a subsidised theatre producing new British plays, international plays and some classical revivals.

The first artistic director George Devine aimed to create a writers' theatre, 'a place where the dramatist is acknowledged as the fundamental creative force in the theatre and where the play is more important than the actors, the director, the designer'. The urgent need was to find a contemporary style in which the play, the acting, direction and design are all combined. He believed that 'the battle will be a long one to continue to create the right conditions for writers to work in'.

Devine aimed to discover 'hard-hitting, uncompromising writers whose plays are stimulating, provocative and exciting'. The Royal Court production of John Osborne's Look Back in Anger in May 1956 is now seen as the decisive starting point of modern British drama and the policy created a new generation of British playwrights. The first wave included John Osborne, Arnold Wesker, John Arden, Ann Jellicoe, N F Simpson and Edward Bond. Early seasons included new international plays by Bertolt Brecht, Eugène Ionesco, Samuel Beckett, Jean-Paul Sartre and Marguerite Duras.

The theatre started with the 400-seat proscenium arch Theatre Downstairs, and in 1969 opened a second theatre, the 60-seat studio Theatre Upstairs. Some productions transfer to the West End, such as Terry Johnson's Hitchcock Blonde, Caryl Churchill's Far Away, Conor McPherson's The Weir, Kevin Elyot's Mouth to Mouth and My Night With Reg. The Royal Court also co-produces plays which have transferred to the West End or toured interna-tionally, such as Sebastian Barry's The Steward of Christendom and Mark Ravenhill's Shopping and Fucking (with Out of Joint), Martin McDonagh's The Beauty Queen Of Leenane (with Druid Theatre Company), Ayub Khan Din's East is East (with Tamasha Theatre Company, and now a feature film).

Since 1994 the Royal Court's artistic policy has again been vigorously directed to finding and producing a new generation of playwrights. The writers include Joe Penhall, Rebecca Prichard, Michael Wynne, Nick Grosso, Judy Upton, Meredith Oakes, Sarah Kane, Anthony Neilson, Judith Johnson, James Stock, Jez Butterworth, Marina Carr, Phyllis Nagy, Simon Block, Martin McDonagh, Mark Ravenhill, Ayub Khan Din, Tamantha Hammerschlag, Jess Walters, Ché Walker, Conor McPherson,

photo: Andy Chopping

Simon Stephens, Richard Bean, Roy Williams, Gary Mitchell, Mick Mahoney, Rebecca Gilman, Christopher Shinn, Kia Corthron, David Gieselmann, Marius von Mayenburg, David Eldridge, Leo Butler, Zinnie Harris, Grae Cleugh, Roland Schimmelpfennig, DeObia Oparei, Vassily Sigarev, the Presnyakov Brothers and Lucy Prebble. This expanded programme of new plays has been made possible through the support of A.SK Theater Projects and the Skirball Foundation, The Jerwood Charity, the American Friends of the Royal Court Theatre and many in association with the Royal National Theatre Studio.

In recent years there have been record-breaking productions at the box office, with capacity houses for Roy Williams' Fallout, Terry Johnson's Hitchcock Blonde, Caryl Churchill's A Number, Jez Butterworth's The Night Heron, Rebecca Gilman's Boy Gets Girl, Kevin Elyot's Mouth to Mouth, David Hare's My Zinc Bed and Conor McPherson's The Weir, which transferred to the West End in October 1998 and ran for nearly two years at the Duke of York's Theatre.

The newly refurbished theatre in Sloane Square opened in February 2000, with a policy still inspired by the first artistic director George Devine. The Royal Court is an international theatre for new plays and new playwrights, and the work shapes contemporary drama in Britain and overseas.

AWARDS FOR ROYAL COURT

Jez Butterworth won the 1995 George Devine Award, the Writers' Guild New Writer of the Year Award, the Evening Standard Award for Most Promising Playwright and the Olivier Award for Best Comedy for Mojo.

The Royal Court was the overall winner of the 1995 Prudential Award for the Arts for creativity, excellence, innovation and accessibility. The Royal Court Theatre Upstairs won the 1995 Peter Brook Empty Space Award for innovation and excellence in theatre.

Michael Wynne won the 1996 Meyer-Whitworth Award for The Knocky. Martin McDonagh won the 1996 George Devine Award, the 1996 Writers' Guild Best Fringe Play Award, the 1996 Critics' Circle Award and the 1996 Evening Standard Award for Most Promising Playwright for The Beauty Queen of Leenane. Marina Carr won the 19th Susan Smith Blackburn Prize (1996/7) for Portia Coughlan. Conor McPherson won the 1997 George Devine Award, the 1997 Critics' Circle Award and the 1997 Evening Standard Award for Most Promising Playwright for The Weir. Ayub Khan Din won the 1997 Writers' Guild Awards for Best West End Play and Writers' Guild New Writer of the Year and the 1996 John Whiting Award for East is East (co-production with Tamasha).

At the 1998 Tony Awards, Martin McDonagh's The Beauty Queen of Leenane (co-production with Druid Theatre Company) won four awards including Garry Hynes for Best Director and was nominated for a further two. Eugene Ionesco's The Chairs (co-production with Theatre de Complicite) was nominated for six Tony awards. David Hare won the 1998 Time Out Live Award for Outstanding Achievement and six awards in New York including the Drama League, Drama Desk and New York Critics Circle Award for Via Dolorosa. Sarah Kane won the 1998 Arts Foundation Fellowship in Playwriting. Rebecca Prichard won the 1998 Critics' Circle Award for Most Promising Playwright for Yard Gal (co-production with Clean Break).

Conor McPherson won the 1999 Olivier Award for Best New Play for The Weir. The Royal Court won the 1999 ITI Award for Excellence in International Theatre. Sarah Kane's Cleansed was judged Best Foreign Language Play in 1999 by Theater Heute in Germany. Gary Mitchell won the 1999 Pearson Best Play Award for Trust. Rebecca Gilman was joint winner of the 1999 George Devine Award and won the 1999 Evening Standard Award for Most Promising Playwright for The Glory of Living.

In 1999, the Royal Court won the European theatre prize New Theatrical Realities, presented at Taormina Arte in Sicily, for its efforts in recent years in discovering and producing the work of young British dramatists.

Roy Williams and Gary Mitchell were joint winners of the George Devine Award 2000 for Most Promising Playwright for Lift Off and The Force of Change respectively. At the Barclays Theatre Awards 2000 presented by the TMA, Richard Wilson won the Best Director Award for David Gieselmann's Mr Kolpert and Jeremy Herbert won the Best Designer Award for Sarah Kane's 4.48 Psychosis. Gary Mitchell won the Evening Standard's Charles Wintour Award 2000 for Most Promising Playwright for The Force of Change. Stephen Jeffreys' I Just Stopped by to See the Man won an AT&T: On Stage Award 2000.

David Eldridge's Under the Blue Sky won the Time Out Live Award 2001 for Best New Play in the West End. Leo Butler won the George Devine Award 2001 for Most Promising Playwright for Redundant. Roy Williams won the Evening Standard's Charles Wintour Award 2001 for Most Promising Playwright for Clubland. Grae Cleugh won the 2001 Olivier Award for Most Promising Playwright for Fucking Games. Richard Bean was joint winner of the George Devine Award 2002 for Most Promising Playwright for Under the Whaleback. Caryl Churchill won the 2002 Evening Standard Award for Best New Play for A Number. Vassily Sigarev won the 2002 Evening Standard Charles Wintour Award for Most Promising Playwright for Plasticine. Ian MacNeil won the 2002 Evening Standard Award for Best Design for A Number and Plasticine. Peter Gill won the 2002 Critics' Circle Award for Best New Play for The York Realist (English Touring Theatre). Ché Walker won the 2003 George Devine Award for Most Promising Playwright for Flesh Wound. Lucy Prebble won the 2003 Critics' Circle Award and the 2004 George Devine Award for Most Promising Playwright for The Sugar Syndrome.

ROYAL COURT BOOKSHOP

The Royal Court bookshop offers a diverse selection of contemporary plays and publications on the theory and practice of modern drama. The staff specialise in assisting with the selection of audition monologues and scenes.
Royal Court playtexts from past and present productions cost £2.
The Bookshop is situated in the downstairs ROYAL COURT BAR AND FOOD.
Monday–Friday 3–10pm, Saturday 2–10pm
For information tel: 020 7565 5024
or email: bookshop@royalcourttheatre.com

PROGRAMME SUPPORTERS

The Royal Court (English Stage Company Ltd) receives its principal funding from Arts Council England, London. It is also supported financially by a wide range of private companies and public bodies and earns the remainder of its income from the box office and its own trading activities. The Royal Borough of Kensington & Chelsea gives an annual grant to the Royal Court Young Writers Programme.
The Genesis Foundation supports the International Season and Young Writers Festival.

The Jerwood Charity supports new plays by new playwrights through the Jerwood New Playwrights series. The Skirball Foundation funds a Playwrights' Programme at the theatre. The Artistic Director's Chair is supported by a lead grant from The Peter Jay Sharp Foundation, contributing to the activities of the Artistic Director's office. Bloomberg Mondays, the Royal Court's reduced price ticket scheme, is supported by Bloomberg. Over the past eight years the BBC has supported the Gerald Chapman Fund for directors.

THE AMERICAN FRIENDS OF THE ROYAL COURT THEATRE

AFRCT support the mission of the Royal Court and is primarily focused on raising funds to enable the theatre to produce new work by emerging American writers. Since this not-for-profit organisation was founded in 1997, AFRCT have contributed to ten productions. They have also supported the participation of young artists in the Royal Court's acclaimed International Residency.

If you would like to support the ongoing work of the Royal Court, please contact the Development Department on 020 7565 5050.

ROYAL COURT
SLOANE SQUARE

Jerwood Theatre Upstairs

24 June –17 July
COUNTRY MUSIC
by **Simon Stephens**

A Royal Court and ATC co-production

Jerwood Theatre Upstairs

Coming this Autumn
YOUNG WRITERS FESTIVAL 2004
A Genesis Project

BOX OFFICE
020 7565 5000
BOOK ONLINE
www.royalcourttheatre.com

SHINING CITY

Conor McPherson

For my wife
Fionnuala

Setting

The play is set in Ian's office in Dublin, around Phibsboro
maybe, or Berkeley Road, an old part of the city which, while
it retains a sense of history, is not a salubrious area. It has a
Victorian feel, lots of redbrick terraced houses dominated by
the Mater hospital, Mountjoy Prison, and the church spires of
Phibsboro Church and the church at Berkeley Road. It doesn't
feel like a suburb, if anything it feels like a less commercial
part of the city centre, which is only a short walk away.

Ian's office is perhaps in an older, larger building than most in
the area, up on the second floor. From his elevated position, at
the back of the building, one or two church spires loom outside.

There is a big sash window at the back. There are some shelves
with books on them. A stereo and some CDs. There are more
books on the floor, as though they have been unpacked but
have yet to be put away. Ian has a desk, stage left-ish, with a
chair behind it. There is also a chair in front of the desk which
Ian uses for sitting with clients. Clients sit on a little two-seater
sofa near the middle of the room, a little more stage right.
There's a coffee table near the sofa with a box of tissues and
a jug of water.

At the back, stage right, is a door to a little toilet. Stage right is
a cabinet of some kind, a filing cabinet maybe, or a bookcase.

The door is stage right, and when it is open we can see out to
the banister and the top of the stairs. Beside the door is a
handset for an intercom to the main door to the street on the
ground floor.

The play has five scenes and about two months elapse between
each scene.

The time is the present.

6

Characters

IAN, *forties*

JOHN, *fifties*

NEASA, *thirties*

LAURENCE, *twenties*

Scene One

*As the lights come up there is no one onstage. It is daytime.
We hear distant church bells. Music is playing softly on the
stereo. We hear the toilet flush, and* IAN, *a man in his forties,
comes out of the bathroom. He takes a tissue from the box and
goes to the window, blowing his nose. He is a man who has
struggled with many personal fears in his life and has had
some victories, some defeats. The resulting struggle has made
him very sharp. He is essentially a gentle man, but sometimes
his desire to get to the lifeboats, to feel safe, drives him in
ways that even he himself doesn't fully understand. A loud ugly
buzzer goes off.* IAN *turns off the stereo and goes to the
intercom, picking up the handset.*

IAN. Hello? (*Pushing a button on the intercom.*) Okay, come in.

    Pause.

    Are you in? Okay. (*Pushing the button.*) Push the door. Are
    you in?

    Pause.

    Hello? No? Okay, okay, hold on.

    *He hangs up the handset and goes out, leaving the door
    open. He goes down the stairs.*

    (*Off.*) Now.

JOHN (*off*). Sorry.

IAN (*off*). No, I'm sorry. Come on up. Yeah. It was fixed.
    I don't know if all this rain . . . We're all the way up, I'm
    afraid.

JOHN (*off*). Straight on?

IAN (*off*). Eh, the next one. Yeah. And that's it there. The door
    is open.

JOHN *comes in. He is in his fifties and dressed quite respectably. He has an air of confusion when we first see him, not just because of his recent experiences but also because he has yet to accept that the world is not as orderly and predictable as he thought. He has always found problems to arise from what he regards as other people's ignorance. He almost regards himself as a benchmark for normality. He carries an anorak. He seems very tired.* IAN *follows him in and indicates for him to have a seat on the sofa.*

IAN. Now, right.

JOHN (*sits*). Thanks.

IAN (*sits*). I'm sorry about that.

JOHN. No, sure I wasn't sure I had the right . . . I was in a bit of a flap, God, the parking around here is horrendous, isn't it?

IAN. I know.

JOHN. I left myself a bit of time but I was almost like a kerbcrawler out there looking for a spot.

IAN. I know. I tell you I'm only here, I've only been here two weeks, and I'm not sure . . . between ourselves . . . that I'm going to . . . (*He nods.*) because there's . . . many disadvantages . . .

JOHN. Ah, no, I parked up in the hospital in the end, which is what I should have done in the first place. I'll know the next time. It's my own fault.

IAN. No, I know, I should have probably . . . But like I say, I'm still sort of only getting myself sorted out here but I should have . . .

JOHN. Ah sure no, it's grand, sure I'm here now.

IAN. Yes! Well good.

JOHN. Yeah, well that's the main thing . . . Can I eh . . . (*indicates water.*)

IAN (*indicates affirmatively*). Please.

JOHN *pours himself some water and drinks a few mouthfuls.* IAN *reaches around behind him and takes a letter from his desk.*

So . . . (*Glancing at letter.*) John . . . (*Pause.*) How are you?

JOHN. Not too bad. A bit . . . Eh . . . heh . . . eh . . . I've never . . . ehm . . . been to see . . . someone before . . .

IAN. Alright. Well that's okay.

JOHN. Em . . . (*He doesn't seem to know where to begin.*)

IAN. I got a, I have a letter . . .

JOHN. Right.

IAN. From Dr Casey . . .

JOHN. That's right. Yeah, he was . . . there was some guy he wanted me to see and . . . we couldn't get an appointment, for four months or something!

IAN. Okay.

JOHN. Yeah, so . . .

IAN. And you haven't been sleeping so well. Is that right?

JOHN. Well, yeah . . .

Pause.

IAN. Which can be very debilitating, I know.

JOHN. Yeah . . . and ehm . . . (*He holds his hand up to the bridge of his nose as though he is about to sneeze and there is silence. He is silently crying.*) Can I . . . ? (*He indicates tissues.*)

IAN. Of course. Please.

JOHN (*composes himself*). Sorry.

IAN (*reassuringly*). That's fine. That's fine.

JOHN. You have the tissues ready and everything.

They smile.

I'm em. I'm recently bereaved. I don't know if Dr Casey . . .

IAN (*affirmative*). Mm hm.

JOHN. My wife passed away a few months ago. And em . . .

> *Pause.*

> She . . . she, she died in em, horrible circumstances, really, you know?

IAN. Okay.

JOHN. She was in a taxi. And a . . . stolen car crashed into them. And she was . . . trapped, in, the car. It was a, a horrific crash, and she . . . didn't, she couldn't survive. And I was on my . . . I was too late getting to the hospital. And the eh . . . reality of . . . the reality of it. It's been absolutely . . . It really, now . . . It's . . . (*He nods.*) You know . . .

> *Pause.*

IAN. I can em . . . I can only imagine what . . .

JOHN. We have no children. And eh . . . (*Pause.*) And I've eh . . . been on my own an awful lot, you know? Like, I've really been on my own an awful lot of the time, really, you know?

IAN. Okay.

JOHN. And I don't . . . I mean I don't even know where she was that night, you know? Or where she was coming from. Do you know what I mean, you know? Like we weren't even . . . communicating. At the time, do you understand me?

IAN. Okay.

JOHN. And no one else was injured. And I've no . . . idea . . . wh . . . (*Long pause.*) But, em, I've . . . em . . . I've seen her. (*Short pause.*) I've em . . .

IAN. Sorry. You've seen her?

JOHN. I've seen her in the house. She's been in the house.

IAN. You've . . .

JOHN. Yeah.

IAN. This is . . .

JOHN. Yeah.

IAN. Since . . .

JOHN. Yeah, since . . .

IAN. Since she . . .

JOHN. Yeah since she . . .

IAN. Sorry, go on . . .

JOHN. Yeah, no, she em . . . about eh, about two months ago.
I . . . met up with my brother, I have a brother, Jim, and we
met one evening, for a pint in Clontarf Castle. We're just,
are we just going into this? You just . . .

IAN. Well, no, just whatever you want, you just tell me . . . in
your own, we don't have to, you can . . . You're telling me
so, I'd like to . . .

JOHN. No I just, I wasn't sure if, but, you know, we . . . my
brother, you know, we don't, we haven't . . . eh . . . I don't
see him. You know, to a certain degree, we've been out of
contact. He only lives in Clontarf. But for . . . you know . . .
he . . . but since the . . . funeral . . . He, you know, we've
had contact again. And it's fine, you know. But for a long
time . . . he's been very supportive, but you know we don't
get on, basically, you know? And I don't . . . there's no need
for me . . . to infringe on his privacy and his family. And
you know, so we've drifted again. But em, the . . . the last
time that I saw him, this night that I'm talking about a
couple of months ago. I mean, I could feel . . . that . . . it
was a sympathy vote, like . . . we'd . . . very little to . . . to
say to each other. And I mean, he's very quiet anyway, you
know? And I . . . didn't feel . . . right, myself that evening,
anyway and . . . And I mean, there was no . . . problem, as
such. But I . . . just wanted to leave, you know? And I kind
of just got a bit annoyed and I kind of . . . fucking . . . just
went home, you know?

He checks with IAN, *to see if this is all alright to continue with.* IAN *nods gently.*

And eh . . .

And I didn't really . . . when I got home, there was nothing untoward when I got in the door. Only that I remember now, because I heard it again, there was the sound, the tune of an ice-cream van. The music, you know? But there couldn't have been because they don't go round at night. But, I heard it when I got in the door. And I . . . didn't think about it or . . . But eh . . . I was, I was just going into the living room and I put the lights on, and . . . when I turned around I could see that she was standing there behind the door looking at me.

Pause.

IAN. Your wife?

JOHN. Yeah. She . . . I could only see half of her, behind the door, looking out at me. Eh . . . but I could see that . . . her hair was soaking wet, and all plastered to her face. And I, I fucking jumped, you know? And I fucking just stood there, I froze, it was terrifying. And I mean she was as real as . . . you know if you've ever seen a dead body? How strange it is, but . . . it's . . . real! That feeling . . .

IAN. And what happened then?

JOHN. I just, I don't know how long we were standing there looking at each other. I mean it might have been only a few seconds. But it was like if you're a kid and you get a fright, it's only for a second, you know, if you have a bad dream or you think you see something, but then, you wake up or there's nothing there or whatever, but this just didn't stop, I mean she was just there, and it was real. The feeling is like . . . I mean, I mean it's unbelievable, you know? It's . . . it's . . . I can't describe it.

IAN. And did she . . . did you . . .

JOHN. Well finally, I don't know how, but I just got my legs going and I just had no choice and I just went straight out the door, straight by her, I mean the door was open, she was behind it, and I just went straight out and right out of the house. (*Pause.*) And then, of course, I was just standing in the garden with no coat on, with really no fucking idea what I was doing, you know? So I just got in the car. (*Pause.*) And I kind of just sat there. Where I live is just a quiet cul-de-sac. There wasn't anyone around even that I could . . . even the neighbours, I've never, you know, those people . . . I just sat there, looking at the house, just so . . . frightened, you know? And . . . there was just nothing I could do. So I just drove away. (*Short pause.*) Just down to this B&B. Bec . . . because I . . . I just didn't want to be on my own like. (*Short pause.*) The woman there, I'd say she knew there was something weird going on alright. I had no luggage and it was so late. She probably thought I'd had a row, you know?

IAN. You didn't go to your brother?

JOHN. No. (*Pause.*) He's . . . we'd, we'd had a . . . I mean I'd walked out on him, earlier, you know? . . . No.

IAN. Did you tell anyone? Is there anyone that you . . . who you . . .

JOHN. No, I . . . I . . . I just . . . I just went back the next day, you know? I . . . I just, I suppose, I made myself, I refused to . . . the next morning it was like, 'What the fuck am I doing?' You know? I mean you just don't know what to do. I rang them in work and said I wouldn't be in, because I sort of knew if I didn't go back . . . I mean when it gets bright you just . . . For some reason I was, I was just able to go back.

IAN. But you didn't talk to anybody about what had happened?

JOHN. No. I suppose I should have but . . .

Silence.

IAN. And did you see . . . her again? Or . . .

JOHN. Yeah, no, well the next time I didn't . . . see anything, I was in the bath, and . . .

IAN. When, how long was this, after . . .

JOHN. Two . . . days later, you know, not long . . .

IAN. Okay.

JOHN. I figured, you know, I, I rationalised it, that maybe . . .
    I hadn't . . . seen her or . . . Like there was nothing there!
    And I thought maybe it . . . that . . . just the fucking grief
    I suppose . . . you know . . .

IAN. Of course.

JOHN. You might say it's mad, but what choice did I have?

IAN. No.

JOHN. I mean, I have to get on with my life!

IAN. I know.

JOHN. So yeah, there I was, having a bath. It was fairly late.
    And I was just trying to relax. I had the radio on. I was
    listening to Vincent Browne. And the door was closed.
    I had . . . I had locked it. It's stupid 'cause there was . . .
    I was there on my own, but, I don't know. It's just a habit
    or it made me feel a bit better, you know, more safe. And I
    was lying there and I thought I, I thought I heard something,
    you know? Like . . . someone in the house. Just not even a
    noise, just a feeling. You can just feel, you know, don't you?
    When someone is there. But I, I just turned off the radio,
    just to see if . . . and then I heard her, she was knocking on
    the door and going . . . (*He bangs his fist urgently on the
    wooden arm of the sofa.*) 'John! John!'

IAN. Oh my God.

JOHN. Yeah! So I, I leapt up out of the bath, and I slipped, and
    I took an awful . . . I went right over and really bruised my
    hip and my shoulder, and by the time I had sorted myself
    out, I got a grip and I . . . eventually, opened the door, but of
    course, and I know you're going to think I was dreaming or
    whatever, there was nothing there. But it was absolutely
    terrifying. And at the same time I was completely frantic,
    do you understand me?

IAN. Well, of course you were. What, what did you . . .

JOHN. Back down to the B&B! What could I do?! (*Pause.*)
I'm still there!

IAN. You're still . . .

JOHN. I'm living there! What can I do?

IAN. I know.

JOHN. I mean I have to sell the house! That's where I'm at,
you know? I'm not working. I'm completely on my own.
I mean the woman in the B&B doesn't know what to make
of me. I mean she's very nice and everything, but what can I
say to her? I told her I'm getting work done. And her husband
is a builder, and he was asking me all these questions one
morning. And I know nothing about it, you know? I think
they think I'm a nutcase!

Silence.

IAN. Okay. (*Pause.*) Well . . .

JOHN. Do you believe me?

IAN (*taking up a writing pad*). Well, let's, let me get some
details, is that alright?

JOHN *nods.*

How old are you, John?

JOHN. Fifty-four.

IAN. And what do you do?

JOHN. I'm a . . . I'm a rep for a catering suppliers . . . on an
independent basis . . .

IAN. And have you . . .

JOHN (*interrupting* IAN). Wait. Do you believe me?

IAN. . . . had any . . . sorry?

JOHN. Do you believe what I'm saying to you? That this is
happening to me?

Pause.

IAN. I believe you . . . that . . . I believe something is . . . I believe you, in that I don't think you're making it up.

JOHN. I'm not making it up.

IAN. Yes but . . . I believe you're telling me you saw something, but if you're asking me if I believe in ghosts, I . . .

JOHN. Yeah but can you help me with this? Because . . . (*His voice suddenly cracks.*) I really don't know what the fuck I'm going to do here . . . (*He puts his hand to his mouth.*)

Pause.

IAN. I know. I know. Don't worry. You're not on your own now, okay? We'll sort it out.

Pause.

Don't worry. (*Short pause.*) Don't worry.

Lights down.

Scene Two

It is night. IAN *and* NEASA *are in the office. Perhaps she sits on the clients' couch. Maybe at the beginning it looks like a therapy session. She is in her thirties and is more working class than* IAN. *She is rooted in a harder, less forgiving reality. She has always had a stubbornness which has kept her focused, but has also sometimes blinded her so that while she is a strong person, often it is others who have used her strength.*

NEASA. Are you fucking joking me, Ian?

IAN. No, I'm . . .

NEASA. No, no no no no no no . . .

IAN. Look, I know, but . . .

NEASA. No no no – (*As though it's so obvious.*) – you come home now.

IAN. Neasa, I'm . . . I'm just not going to do that.

He goes to the desk and takes a cigarette from a pack.

NEASA. No. Because people have fights, Ian, and everybody hates it – but you know you have to do it sometimes, you know? That's . . . Please don't smoke, Ian, 'cause it'll make me want to smoke.

IAN. Okay! What's that smell?

NEASA. It's new . . . stuff for the . . . thing . . . on my leg.

IAN (*beat*). And this is not because we had a fight! What do you think I am?! I know that people have fights – this is not because . . . It's not because I'm 'hurt' or something – it's, it's because . . .

NEASA. Oh, it's not because you're hurt, no? It's not because you're sulking and you've been letting me stew in my own juice for four days, no?

IAN. No I haven't actually – I've been trying to just fucking think about what I need to figure out what I need to do, you know?

NEASA. But you couldn't phone me, to tell me that, no? You just let . . . me just . . .

IAN (*shouts*). Anytime I thought about phoning you I knew that it would just turn into this! We said, both of us said that we should give it a bit of time to . . . but oh no . . .

NEASA (*shouts*). I didn't know you were going to leave me on my own for a whole week, and I didn't even know where you were!

IAN. It's not a week, it's a couple of days, Jesus!

NEASA. It's not just a couple of days when you're on your own with a baby – it's completely fucking exhausting not knowing where you are – and I can't fucking do it!

What am I supposed to say to your brother? He hasn't even asked me where you are! No one knows what to say – of course – she's delighted – she hates me – they think I've ruined your life. She's delighted with herself that I'm sitting up there on my own – she's so fucking smug now!

IAN (*annoyed, embarrassed, dismissive*). It doesn't matter what they think.

NEASA. That's easy for you to say! I have nowhere to fucking go! It's their house! What right do I have to stay there if you're not there?

IAN. It's none of their business!

NEASA. What do you mean it's none of their business? You don't know what it's like! I'm sitting up there on my own in the boxroom with the baby, they don't even come near me. And I can't go downstairs! You should have seen the face on her when I asked her to mind Aisling tonight! (*Shouts.*) You don't know what it's like!

IAN. Look! This is all . . . getting sorted out! I nearly have a thousand euros in the bank – if you just let me get on with my work, if you just let me do it my way, you'll have your own place, there'll be no more of this and we can get on with it, but if you're going to . . . (*Unsaid: 'harass me'.*) I can't . . . (*Unsaid: 'work'.*)

NEASA. What do you mean, my own place?

IAN. Can you not see that this is happening!? I don't . . . want . . . I can't . . . I can't . . . I can't . . . I don't . . . I don't want this relationship anymore!

NEASA. What the fuck are you talking about? What the *fuck* are you talking about?

IAN. God! Can you not hear me?! Can you not listen to what I'm saying?

NEASA. I don't know if I can! Because have you completely lost touch with reality? Have you completely fucking lost touch with fucking reality?

IAN. This is reality!!

NEASA. What are you talking about? What about the baby?!

IAN. But this is not about the baby!

NEASA. What are you talk . . . How can it not be about the baby?!

IAN (*shouts*). Because it's not about that! Because it's about that *I* can't continue with *you*! With you and me!

NEASA. But what do you mean? What have I done? What have I done?

IAN. It's not what you've *done* or what I've *done*. It's . . . It's . . .

NEASA. What . . . What, Ian . . .

IAN. IT'S BECAUSE I CAN'T DO IT!

Pause.

NEASA. I knew this. I knew this was going to happen. I knew it. I knew it.

IAN. Look, if you'd just listen to me for once, and hear
something that goes in, we're going to get you out of my
brother's house. It's all going to be sorted out and I'm
earning some money now and everything.

NEASA. Yeah, now that it's all . . . Now you're on your feet.
My father fucking said this to me, you know? He fucking
said it to me. A priest . . . ?

IAN. I'm not a . . . !!

NEASA. An ex-priest? Forget it – he said anyone who goes
next or near the priests is a fucking headcase to begin with.
But I wouldn't listen to him!

IAN. Oh yeah, and your dad is a real one to know.

NEASA. Yeah, he's a drunk. But he's a human being, you
know? He has feelings – he knows things, you know?

IAN. Yeah, well, is your father going to find you somewhere to
live?

NEASA. Oh yeah, like you really found us somewhere to live,
Ian. Squashed into your brother's house with that fucking
bitch always fucking looking at me like I'm going to rob
something, like she has anything . . .

IAN. Wait, now, don't fucking . . . What did you think was
going to fucking happen?! I said it to you, I have to start all
over again and it's gonna be tough! (*Sarcastic.*) Of course
you didn't know that – you didn't know any of that!

NEASA. Yeah but I didn't think that at the end of it all you
were . . . (*Despair, bewilderment.*) Are you breaking it off
with me!? (*Pause.*) I was just thinking about it. Do you
remember the week you left the order – about . . . a day
later, you were so worried about money, I'd say like a *day*
later – I *immediately* started working all the extra shifts I
could get. I kept having to lick up to that sleazy bollocks
Darren, just to keep working in that fucking *kip* of a pub . . .

IAN. Look, I know, I know that.

NEASA. Just so you wouldn't have to worry about anything!
No one could understand how I put up with the things that

he said to me in front of people. But I did it so you could
have the money for your course!

IAN. I know. I know. And . . . look . . . I'm . . . going to do
everything that I can. And, I promise, I'm going to look
after you, you know?

NEASA (*shouts*). But I don't want for you to 'look after' me!
I never wanted for anyone to have to look after me! I even
said – when I got pregnant – I even said then we should leave
it and we should wait until we have some more money –
I said, 'This is too soon.' YOU SAID, 'NO', YOU SAID,
'NO, NOT TO DO THAT!' Because you thought it was
'wrong'! Now look! (*Short pause.*) What am I going to do?
How can I go back there on my own again tonight? What
am I going to say to your brother?

IAN. Don't say anything to him. I'll talk to him.

She stands there. She is ruined. Pause.

NEASA. What am I going to do?

IAN. Can you not go back around to your granny, even for a
few . . . ?

NEASA. My dad is back there!

IAN *throws his eyes to heaven as if this is an endless
saga . . .*

IAN. Look, I know. I know that this . . . seems . . . like . . .
but . . . this is the worst point, you know? And I've . . .
I know I've made some huge mistakes, and I'm the first
person who'll say that, you know? But I've got to put it
right, and I'm going to put it right. But we can't continue
like this and . . .

NEASA. Ian, I don't think I can do this on my own. I didn't
think that this was going to happen.

IAN. I know but . . . you're not on your own. I'm with you in
this, you know?

NEASA. But what are you saying to me?

IAN (*calmly, reasonably, almost sweetly*). Look. Aisling is our daughter. And I'm her father and you're her mother. And I fully . . . you know? I want to be her father and . . . be, you know . . . but you and I . . . are breaking up. And that's all, you know? That's all that's happening here. That's all it is.

NEASA. How can you say that? How can you say that that's all it is? Can you see what this is doing to me?

IAN. I know. But we can't . . . I . . . can't . . .

NEASA. Do you not love me anymore?

IAN. I . . . I'll always . . . . I mean, you have been . . . you were the only . . . when . . . when it was all so hard for me . . . And I had to make that big decision – and it was a *huge* thing for me – (*as though he has accomplished something completely unthinkable*) – to turn my back on the church?! – that was a *huge* thing for me. You were there for me, and I couldn't have come through it without you. I just couldn't have done it, I just couldn't have, you know? But . . . the fucking huge mistake I made was thinking that that was the end of the journey for me – and it wasn't.

Pause.

NEASA. Have you met somebody else?

IAN. No, no I haven't. I promise you. It's not that . . . (*Pause.*) I can't stay with you, with us, I can't do it. But I'm going to make sure that you want for nothing.

NEASA. But I just don't understand any of this. I just can't believe that it's happening even, you know?

She takes a bottle of wine from her bag.

I bought this this afternoon because I thought we were going to make up, and then you were going to come home with me.

She is shaking with fear and dread.

IAN. I'm sorry. I'm sorry. I'm sorry.

Silence.

NEASA. Is this . . . Is this because of me and Mark Whelan?

IAN. What?

Pause.

NEASA. Is it because . . .

IAN. Because what? (*Pause.*) Because what? (*Pause.*) What do you, what are you . . . ?

NEASA. Look, it doesn't matter, okay? Forget I asked.

IAN. No, wait, hold on. What do you mean is this because of you and Mark Whelan? What about you and Mark Whelan?

NEASA. Please, Ian, just . . . Please . . .

IAN. What do you mean it doesn't matter? What doesn't matter?

NEASA. Nothing, just . . . because I wanted just to ask you . . . if that was why.

IAN. But why are you asking me that? Did you . . .

NEASA. Ian, please, I'm asking you not to ask me about this now, please!

IAN. Not to ask you about what though?

Pause.

Not to ask you about what?

Pause.

I'm not . . . (*Unsaid: 'surprised'.*) Because, do you remember, I asked you about him before.

NEASA. And I told you.

IAN. You said there was nothing going on!

NEASA. There wasn't . . . then, when . . .

IAN. So what? Have you something you want to tell me?

NEASA. It doesn't make any difference, Ian, please, believe me. I just wanted to know if it was because . . .

IAN. Yeah, but, like I mean, what?

NEASA. Please, Ian. Please, I'm asking you, okay?

IAN. Yeah, but . . . I mean . . . wait a minute . . . What about you and Mark Whelan, you know? (*Pause.*) Have you had sex with him?

Pause. She doesn't know what to say – all she knows is that it feels like her world is ending.

That's a 'yes' then, I suppose then, yeah?

Pause.

NEASA. Can you not see what this is doing to me, Ian? Can you not see what this is doing to me? You're doing it anyway, Ian, you're leaving me anyway. Please don't leave me, please don't do it.

IAN knows that he shouldn't continue with this, but he can't help it. He feels angry, frightened, powerless, but also adrenalised.

IAN. Yeah, but you know what? This is fucking . . . You're throwing the baby in my face . . . and you're screwing around!

NEASA. I'm not!

IAN. But it's like I'm the one who, you know, that I . . .

NEASA. It was before the baby, Ian, I wasn't screwing around!

IAN. When before the baby? Just before?

NEASA. No, she's our baby Ian, no!

IAN. Is she? I mean, wh . . . because I don't *know* . . . anything, here.

Pause.

Because I was shocked when you got pregnant, we both were. I thought we both were.

NEASA. No, no no no, she's your baby, she's your baby, she's yours and mine – this is crazy! Just, you have to believe me. Don't even . . .

IAN. Look, wait, hold on, hold on. This is . . . What are we talking about here?

Pause.

NEASA. Nothing. Really. Nothing. There was just . . . no one to talk to and . . .

IAN (*interrupting*). When?

NEASA. Just in, all around that time. When you came out and you were freaked out all the time, and you were starting your course. And I was working all the time. I just couldn't . . . keep going back up to your brother's house on my break, with her always there, Ian, it was horrible.

IAN. You know they've been so good to us really when you think about it, you know that?

NEASA. I know but, I was just always on my own!

IAN. But you weren't! When?

NEASA. I just . . . I didn't have anyone even that I could just have a normal talk to.

Pause.

I just feel like it's all my fault now, you know? And I was . . . I was worried all the time about everything, even then, you know? Mark just, would always ask me if I was alright, and how I was getting on . . .

IAN. Oh, I never asked you how you were? I'm just a fucking animal, yeah?

NEASA. I just believed him, when he asked.

Pause.

IAN (*dismissive*). Yeah, well.

NEASA. I didn't know what was going on. It was just like things were supposed to get better and they just kept getting worse and worse. I couldn't go back up there on my break. She always was saying something about the smell of smoke off me. I was working in a pub! You know? What did she

want me to do? And . . . I started going around to Mark's
flat – I told you, I told you I was doing that.

IAN. Yeah but . . .

NEASA. Yeah, well, I didn't . . . I didn't know that . . .
anything . . . was . . . going to happen. I didn't think that
there was even anything like that with him . . . But one day
he was . . . he didn't say anything to me . . . We just got in
the door and I just knew that . . . what he was . . . I didn't
know what to do. I just, I only kind of realised when we got
in the door that . . . he was . . . It was just really, I didn't . . .
it was just really quick and it was, I didn't even want to do
it. We both felt terrible after it. I'm sorry, Ian. I'm sorry. It
was only once. It was only one time. It wasn't anything,
really. And I've never gone there after.

I'm sorry, Ian.

I don't love him, Ian. I never loved him. I only ever wanted
to be with you. Really. Really.

And I don't know what happened.

Say something. Say something to me, will you?

Long pause.

IAN. I'm sorry.

Silence.

NEASA *starts to get her stuff together. She leaves the bottle
of wine.*

NEASA. I better go. 'Cause I'm gonna miss the last bus.

IAN. Look. I'll . . . I'll call you tomorrow, and . . .

NEASA (*almost silently*). Yeah.

She goes to the door.

IAN. Neasa.

She pauses.

Look, I'm . . .

Pause.

NEASA. It's not your fault.

She leaves. He stands there.

Lights down.

Scene Three

Lights up on the office. It is the afternoon, six or eight weeks later. The door is open and there is no one in the office. There is a bit more furniture around the place, maybe a plant or two. JOHN comes in and stands there. He looks a bit better than he did in Scene One, and there is something more focused about him, he means business. IAN follows him in.

IAN (*slightly exasperated*). Well, I don't know . . .

JOHN. I'm sorry, God, I can never . . .

IAN. No! You know I've asked them every single week, and they say they have a caretaker who keeps missing me. I think it's a total spoof.

JOHN. Don't give them the rent.

IAN. You think?

JOHN. They'll be round in a flash. That's the language they speak, you know. Money talks in this town. It rules really, you know?

IAN. God, tell me about it! Keeps me fit anyway, going up and down the stairs.

JOHN. Yeah! Well . . .

JOHN really has his bearings in the office now. He throws his jacket over a chair and sits, unbidden, on the sofa, pouring himself a glass of water. IAN sits.

IAN. So . . . how are you?

JOHN. Yeah, well I'm . . . this helps, you know . . .

IAN. Good, good . . .

JOHN. I, you know, I focus around it. It's been a good week em . . . They're, you know still very good about everything at work, there's no pressure to go in . . . em . . . the time is . . . good . . . it's . . .

Pause.

IAN. Are you sleeping or . . .

JOHN. Well, the same really. You know, I do . . . get a few hours. But, it's like there's something in me's determined to keep me up all night, you know? I never go off till around five, six, even. Then, of course, nine o'clock, the woman knocks on the door so I won't 'miss breakfast'. God forbid! You know?

They smile.

So . . . of course I'm in bits but, I get up, go down. I'm always the last. She usually has a few staying there, but, they're on business or whatever, they're . . . they're gone out, you know? So, I sit there, watching the traffic outside, and . . . I have an egg, cup of coffee . . . Get myself going then . . . you know . . .

IAN. You're still getting your walk in . . .

JOHN. Rain or shine. I get out, go down the coast. Down as far as the Bull Wall. The B&B is more the Fairview end so, you know, it's a good walk . . . Get the paper, throw any stuff into the laundry there. There's a little café next door, there near the Dollymount House. So, you know . . . that's . . . been the little routine, but I've em . . . I've bitten the bullet and done what you suggested. Couple of mornings I got in the car, dropped into the house, you know?

IAN. Okay. So, how is that?

JOHN. It's okay, you know, it's okay. (*Pause.*) So quiet, obviously . . . but I . . . did, I do what you say, and I focus on eh, a small, objective. I stay . . . (*Unsaid*: '*centered on it*'.) There were a couple of bills there, or whatever, there on the mat. Okay. Down to the Post Office, paid that . . . Em . . .

Pause.

IAN. And how does it feel in the house? When you're there.

JOHN. In the house, itself? Like I say. I'm aware, I'm wary . . .
but in a funny way I . . . I can't . . . I can . . . hardly accept
what I saw . . . you know . . . But, I know that I did, and so,
obviously . . .

IAN. You're a little . . .

JOHN. I'm a little uneasy.

IAN (*nods*). Okay.

JOHN. But that's . . . that's also to do with . . . Like, when
Mari was alive, you know, we had . . . stopped communicating. But now . . . she's gone, I really feel like there was a
lot of communication. Even though, it wasn't . . . verbal . . .
I suppose. I mean, she was there. And I was there. And in
that, there's obviously, the presence of . . . you know, a
living person, I'm not saying this very well. But I think, you
know, I believe that . . . we had a huge importance in each
other's lives. You know?

IAN. I don't doubt it for a second.

JOHN (*very affirmative*). Yeah. (*Beat.*) Yeah. I know.

Pause.

You know, when you're young. And you're told about . . .
what to expect I suppose. It is kind of happy ever after. But
it's . . . you know, it's weird to accept what happiness really
is, you know, or what it is . . . nothing is ever like anyone
expects, is it, you know? Like, it's not a fairy tale . . . I
mean, it has to be just kind of ordinary, you know? A bit
boring even, otherwise it's probably not real, you know?

IAN. . . . Yeah . . . ?

JOHN. No, it's, it's just that . . . we probably had it, you
know? I mean when I think of it, really, we . . . we had it
all, you know? But it's, it's hard to . . . accept . . . that this
is it. You . . . you go . . . searching, not *searching*, I wasn't
going anywhere searching for anything, but, I think I was
always slightly . . . waiting . . . you know?

This is something I probably wouldn't even have admitted
before, you know? But maybe I felt that when we were

married, and all settled in and eh . . . maybe even before we
found out that we couldn't, that Mari couldn't, have
children, I think that maybe even before that . . . I felt that I
had kind of settled for second best, you know? I mean I
mean I look at it now, and man, these are old feelings. Just
fucking there all the time, for . . . all the way along.

Silence.

That's terrible, isn't it?

IAN. You felt what you felt . . .

JOHN (*slight self-disgust*). Yeah but, what . . . who the fuck
did I think I was? You know?

Pause.

You see, we'd, I think, we'd been slightly left behind, a
little bit, you know? All our . . . all our friends, they, you
know, they had families. And, that . . . that . . . bound them
together, you know? And, you see, I think that that . . . that
we were . . . we were slightly left behind a little bit maybe.
And that we felt that there was something kind of wrong
with us, not anything serious or really wrong, but that there
was a whole . . . you know, a whole experience, a whole
way, maybe, of . . . of relating to everything, that wasn't . . .
it wasn't available to us. (*Suddenly.*) It was a pain in the
fucking hole to tell you the truth!

You know. I don't know if you have children, and I don't
mean anything, because this is nothing about those people,
but you know, I found, we found, that, okay, of course we
were invited to places, you know, to parties and everything.
But that's what there was to talk about, you know? 'Oh my
sons are ten and eleven.' 'Oh my son is eleven!' You know?

And of course! Look, that's what people talk about. Of
course they do. It's perfectly normal to want to talk about
the things that are happening in your life. But, you know,
that was what we were always sort of on the edge of. You
know, those conversations. You know, you'd be trying to,
waiting for the subject to change and then of course, some
stupid fucker would turn around and go, 'Do you have any

kids, yourself, John?' And I'd be, and I know that this
happened to Mari too, I'd be like, 'Eh, no, no actually, I
don't.' Which'd be then . . . 'Oh! Right! Okay!' You know?

I mean, I don't know if it felt like a big thing at the time, in
a funny way, but it must have been, because I always felt . . .
that it . . . wasn't . . . addressed because in a way, maybe
I felt that the whole thing should be different – not just that
we should adopt some kid or something – but that I should
change the whole . . . the whole fucking thing, you know?
Start again, somewhere else. Which then, of course, just
feels mad and you want to let yourself believe that all these
things aren't that important but . . . it was there and . . . what
can I say? There was all this shit going on and I . . . our life
just carried on and we grew up basically and our child-
bearing years were over and we got on with it, and that's,
but then, out the fucking blue, about three years ago . . .

Pause.

I met someone, you know?

Pause.

I mean . . . I didn't meet her, we'd already met her, we both
had met her, up at a . . . party up there in Howth up there,
you know? House of a guy I was doing some business with.

(*Suddenly.*) This is fucking mad fucking shit, now, you know?

IAN. I know. I know. It's okay . . .

JOHN. Yeah, well, like I say it was someone we'd both seen
around a little bit for years. She's wealthy, you know? The
husband is loaded, you know? And I suppose just the
ordinary feelings of that . . . surface . . . glamour . . . I mean
you'd see this woman, there was no doubt about it, she was,
you know, the most beautiful woman in the room or
whatever, or even wherever you'd go she'd be one of the top
five best-looking women there, you know? I mean, that's
what we're talking about here, you know? And obviously
that's . . . that's very attractive, you know?

But about three years ago we were invited up to this guy,
O'Leary, big hotel guy, up to his mansion up there on

Howth Head. And both of us were excited about it and looking forward to it, you know, Mari liked, dressing up. She had a good figure and she could, she could definitely hold her own, and this would have been a big deal and we were in good form going up there beforehand. And it was, you know, there were people up there parking the cars for you and all this, you know what I mean? Up these steps like, and butlers standing there with champagne and hot ports and all this, serious stuff now, you know?

And in we go, into this place, serious mansion now, you know? And as usual, you know, we're fucking standing there on our own – fucking, you know, trying to talk to each other, but of course we both wanted to get stuck in and meet some other people and I was dying for a slash and Mari doesn't want to let me go and leave her on her own there, and all that, yeah?

But eventually we get talking to another couple, and a business guy I know comes in and it's warming up and I leg it down to the jacks and kind of – the way it goes, you know, I don't see Mari until everyone sits down later on for something to eat, 'cause when I'm coming out of the toilet and I'm going through the kitchen I meet a few other people who are there, and then I meet this . . . this woman that I'm talking about . . .

Her name is Vivien . . .

And I stop and say hello and, you know, we're standing there at the . . . you know, in the middle of a kitchen, sometimes in those big houses . . .

IAN. An island.

JOHN. Yeah, and there were these stools and it was like we were sitting at a bar somewhere, you know? The champagne keeps coming round, and it's great, you know? Because not only is this woman so beautiful to look at but we're having a brilliant chat, you know? 'Cause I had been in hospital for a few days having this thing done on my sinuses and it was weird because she was asking me about it and no one had asked me anything really, you know, not even Mari,

although she had been great and everything and she came to
see me every day – but I'd felt just this . . . just this real
lonely feeling when I was in there, you know? I don't know
why, or what happened but when I was in there, I just felt a
bit scared and . . . and em . . .

But I'd had these feelings and anyway, for some reason I
mentioned this to . . . to Vivien, and you know, God it just
felt like I was being taken seriously. You know, and the
champagne is coming round and it turns out that Vivien was
in hospital at nearly the same time, you know? And she
starts telling me that . . . she'd had . . . a miscarriage, you
know? And she's telling me all this and she already has four
kids who are teenagers and this pregnancy was out of the
blue, and there'd been all this going on, and it hadn't
worked out, and all this had . . . you know brought up, a lot
of things for her about many things in her life and it's all
this and, so like we're having this big talk, and then, you
know, it's an hour-and-a-half later, and we're all being called
in to sit down at this huge dinner . . . and on the way in,
she . . . she takes my mobile number and puts it in her phone.
And although in one way it just seemed like a normal
thing to do, in another it was . . . you know . . . and I didn't
really . . . let on to Mari that I'd only been talking to Vivien
all that time when I got back, you know, I played up the
other people that I'd only seen or just said hello to.

So we're there and we don't have a great time, because Mari
is pissed off that I'd left her talking to these fuckers she
didn't really know, and of course, about twelve o'clock, she
says she doesn't feel so good, so great! We're the first ones
to leave and we're not talking in the car and it's basically
just one of those, and I'm kind of used to it, you know?

But Christmas, you know, we go over to her folks' house
and do the whole bit, and when I get home, bit tipsy, I'm
upstairs getting changed and I see on my phone, I have a
text. And it's from Vivien and it's, 'Great to see you the
other night. Happy Christmas.'

So I'm like standing up there in the bedroom, in my socks,
you know, and I'm like some youngfella, and I text her

back, 'It was great to see you too,' you know, 'Happy
Christmas.'

And some part of me knew, you know? That I was sort of
going into something . . . you know? And . . .

Pause.

But, you know there were no more texts and . . . but,
something had . . . I mean whatever it triggered off . . . you
know . . . here I was all of a sudden, just really thinking
about this woman. Who . . . in many ways was different to
what I knew, you know? And probably the big one was . . .
you know . . . that . . . She was a mother.

Whatever that . . . means, you know? But anyway,
Christmas was gone, and the new year and all that bollocks,
which is a very depressing time of the year as far as I'm
concerned and there were no more texts . . . and . . . I don't
know what I was expecting to happen but I just got more
and more into a filthy mood, over those days. And Mari was
asking me what was wrong with me, and I was bulling
because I'd erased Vivien's text, and I wanted to look at it
again as something to hang on to, which was you know,
whatever.

But as usual, Mari dragged me into the Christmas sales
because I needed new clothes and we were in fucking . . .
Roches Stores or somewhere and . . . I got a text . . . from
Vivien, and it was just like, 'How are you?' You know? And
man, it was like someone had thrown me a rope, you know?
I was like, 'Thank God!' You know? There's someone in the
world who actually cares about how I'm getting on, you
know? Like, this was what that meant to me. Crazy fucking
shit, you know?

So I slipped off and said I wanted to have a look at some
shoes or something, and I texted her back, quickly just
saying 'Post-Xmas blues,' or something and bang! She
texted me right back like, 'Hang in there,' or something and
that's, it's so fucking stupid, but that's how it continued then
all day really.

IAN. Your wife didn't hear all these texts going off?

JOHN (*shakes his head*). No, I had the phone on silent, vibrate, in my pocket, you know? I mean, you know? I was already . . . you know . . . ?

IAN. Mm. Yeah I know.

JOHN. And of course, suddenly I'm all chipper then, and I take Mari for her lunch in the Westbury! You know, I'm all cheered up. That morning she'd seen this bright red coat in one of the designer shops in Brown Thomas or somewhere. Reduced from like three grand to two grand or something, and of course it was still too dear and all that, but after lunch I took her down and bought it for her, you know? The fucking guilt, you know?

I mean, this is the terrible side of it. That coat was then, like her good coat from then on, you know?

Pause.

She was wearing it, you know, the night she was . . . the night she died, you know?

Pause.

She had it on when I saw her, you know? Behind the door there.

He exhales deeply.

So, but, you know, we went home, life continues. Back to work, which I was glad about, because, you know, it gave me more time to myself. You know? Texting Vivien? You know?

IAN. Mmm.

JOHN. And then of course . . .

IAN. What were the texts?

JOHN. Ah, it was just normal stuff, you know? Nothing. 'How are you doing?' 'Back to work today.' 'Ah well, keep your chin up!' You know? Nothing – except that it shouldn't have been happening . . . you know, so . . . so then, of course, as time goes on, that's, that's not enough for me . . . ? So . . . I, I text her and say, 'Let's have a coffee sometime.' And

that's opened it up, because, at first I hear nothing, and
I think, 'Woah, I've gone to far . . . ' But then bang! Like a
day later . . . She fucking rings me! Right in the middle of
a meeting with these two business guys down in Longford,
in the Longford Arms Hotel. And I see her name come up
on the phone – so I'm like, 'I have to take this.' So I go
outside and it's like, 'God it's great to hear you', you know?
It was just . . . it just felt like such a fucking relief, you
know?

And she's on for like a big chat on the phone, but I'm like . . .
I can't do it, so I kind of cut to the chase, and I say, 'Let's
meet up!' you know? And she's, you know, suddenly I sense
a kind of reluctance, like she's not saying no, but . . . I can
just . . . (*Unsaid: 'sense it'*.) But I drive it on and I say, 'Let's
meet on Friday, get some lunch, just get a quick sandwich
somewhere', or something, and she's like, 'Where?' And so
like, without either of us acknowledging it, I say, 'The
Killiney Court Hotel', because it's really miles out of the
way for both of us, and no one would see us, you know, but
of course I don't say that, but I figure she gets it, and I say
I'm going to be out that way and so on. All very innocent,
like – (*Sarcastic.*) 'Yeah, right!' But my heart was pounding
while I'm talking to her, you know? And I could . . . like the
stakes were really going up!

IAN (*affirmative*). Well, yeah . . .

JOHN. And . . . I mean, I don't know if you know what it's
like, but . . . Having a secret like that from your wife . . .
Nothing is as strong as a secret like that, I mean for binding
two people. In my *mind* anyway! As far as I was concerned,
we were already like two fugitives or something, you know?
So, but, we made this arrangement. And of course, the next
few days was kind of mad, like, 'What am I doing?', 'This
is crazy.' I was . . . I was just like an actor, or something,
in my own life, just playing this part in something that just
didn't seem real, you know, or as real as . . . I mean, crazy,
you know? Like I felt I could just look behind everything
because it was only scenery, everywhere I went. Because,
I suppose in a mad way I believed that *something else* was
my reality! And that all this other shit – my life! – was . . .

Like I found myself looking at Mari while she was prattling on and thinking, 'Who the fuck is this fucking woman?' What's happened? That we live in the same house? There's been some fucking . . . mistake, you know?

IAN (*affirmative*). Mmm.

JOHN. So a few days later, Friday, you know, I had cleared the decks, I had nothing else to do so I was over there in Killiney at like twelve o'clock, you know? And it was a horrible day, you know? It never really got bright – didn't rain, but it was . . . almost like GOD KNOWS WHAT YOU'RE DOING . . . you know?

They both laugh a little.

And eh . . . we met, you know? (*Suddenly without any defence or guile.*) I couldn't believe it when I saw her coming through the door. I just could not fucking believe it, you know? I was like, Thank God, you know? Like how can this beautiful woman be coming in here to be with me? You know? This is *real*, you know? God. And she just came in there and she sat down where I was sitting. And she was really nervous too, you know? And she just starts talking, talking, talking. Her kid is in this new school and all this, and her husband is going through this huge deal at work and he's in Japan all the time and she's getting this work done by these builders, and basically all this bollocks that I realise I have no interest in at all! And there was this horrible feeling that all this going on and on was just really a bit annoying, you know? This just wasn't . . . I was selfish basically, and I . . . I wanted this to be more about me, you know?!

They smile.

So we got a few hot whiskeys and after I feel like I've been politely listening to all this shite for long enough, I started to move it around more to . . . us being there, and . . . and I knew I was rushing it but . . . I was really just, trying to move it on to the next stage. Because I didn't want the whole . . . illusion of it . . . wrecked. I mean, I was putting everything into this – the whole lot – all the eggs in the one basket, I mean, insane, you know?

And I mean, madly, I just said to her, 'Look I need to . . . be with you, you know? And hold you and . . . ' Crazy.

And she just went so quiet then that I thought, okay, I've fucked it, you know, she's . . . you know, she thought this was something else . . . like we were going to be just friends in some . . . bizarre way I don't fucking . . . relate to, you know? And it was three o'clock now and I'd have to start heading soon now anyway, but then she goes, 'Yeah, okay, let's . . . ' But then I'm like slightly, like 'Don't just do this for me!' You know, like, don't kill yourself . . . But sure, I didn't even know what I was doing, you know?

I was like a robot. But everything I was doing was wrong so nothing made sense, like I got the key, and I was convinced your woman behind the desk was going to call the fucking guards, you know?! And this was before that place closed down, it was between when they had sold it and when they closed it down, there was hardly anyone around. Going up to the room, you know? And we didn't say anything. It was just, it was just . . . frightening really. And we go in and the room was like . . . it was like walking into one of the rooms in Fawlty Towers or something, like it was straight out of the 1970s. All brown and pink flowery patterns everywhere. And it was freezing. It was . . . it was horrible.

But. We sat on the bed. And we . . . started . . . sort of . . . kissing, but, I wasn't . . . it was just so obvious that this wasn't what she wanted. And to tell you the truth I was completely out of practice and I . . . tried to put my hand up her skirt and . . . you know, but she just stopped me. And neither of us were . . . it was just a huge mistake. I had fucked the whole thing to hell, really, you know? And I wanted to just go back to before, when we were just going to meet, you know?

But I didn't . . . I wasn't able to . . . quite express that, so . . . I was just sort of apologising, and really, we both had to go then and . . .

It was just fucking awful to tell you the truth, and there didn't seem to even be time to . . . make it . . . like, to have a drink and work it out or make it okay again. It was just

over and we just, said goodbye in the car park, you know?
Brilliant.

And of course when I got home, just the distance that I felt
between me and Mari, I realised that whatever about the
way we might have been before, it was nothing compared to
this. This was like the Grand Canyon opening up, you
know? I knew that I'd driven an unbelievable wedge . . .
between us.

And of course, Mari can tell there's something wrong and
she's . . . asking me, is there anything she can . . . She came
and started stroking my back saying, 'God, those are big
heavy sighs, John.' You know? So I just said, 'Ah it's a thing
at work, don't worry about it.' Whatever, you know?

But seriously, you know, as the days went on, I mean I
wasn't getting any sleep, and I was getting up in the middle
of the night and just sitting in the kitchen, and then, not able
to go into work.

Pause.

It was just so . . . I just felt like a piece of shit, you know?

I mean, I had gone from sharing this – I suppose it was a
dream – of a . . . special communication or a secret . . .
relationship that . . . and now it was, I mean I just felt like
some sort of criminal. And I really felt so isolated and cut
off and like there was nothing in my life to look forward to.
And I just felt like, I knew then that something bad was
going to happen, because I deserved it, because there was
like some kind of evil in me, that I did.

IAN. Mari didn't . . . you didn't . . .

JOHN. Well, she just didn't know what to do, because I was
just only, barely communicating with her. Because I fucking
hate myself by this stage, you know?

And when I think about what I must have done to her. With
all the silence and . . .

Pause.

I started pretending I had to stay down the country, for
work, you know, overnight, but I was really just staying in

places just so that I didn't have to deal with the terrible *pressure* of going home, you know? And facing that, and facing myself, and, you know?

I'd just be sitting there in some hotel bar in the midlands, you know? Just smoking cigarettes and looking at football or Man United or whatever – just unable to deal with anything, really. And I just, I had been staying in this place in Kildare and I had to leave and come back to Dublin, because I could only ever justify staying away for a night or possibly two at a push, and I was having a cup of coffee before I hit the road and I picked up this magazine, in a whole rack of old magazines, and I saw an ad for like, an escort service, a brothel. I knew what it was. And . . . I just needed to . . . connect with something, or someone, you know? When you're so alone like that . . . and when you feel . . . you know . . . I just . . . I just dialled the number and this woman answered and she sounded so nice, and you know, she told me where to go. To this place on the South Circular Road. And I fucking drove there, you know? I just . . .

Long pause.

IAN. Are you okay?

JOHN. Yeah, it's just, this is terrible.

IAN. No.

JOHN. I just find it so fucking hard . . .

IAN. You're doing so well, John. This is such important work, you know?

Pause.

Do you want to leave it there? We can just sit for a while . . . ?

JOHN. How's the time, are we finished?

IAN. No we have time, but maybe you'd just prefer to . . .

JOHN. Well . . . No, I'll, I'll finish what I . . . I came . . . today to . . . you know . . .

IAN. Okay.

JOHN. Yeah, so I eh . . . anyway, I went to this place. Which was something I had never done. And this woman answered the door, and I was hoping the minute I saw her that she wasn't, I mean, she was a bit older now . . . And she brought me into this room. And there was just a couch there, and a shower over in one corner and some towels on a chair, and she says that this girl, Jeanette, was going to come in in a minute. And she says it's thirty euros to be there and then whatever I work out with Jeanette is between ourselves. And I mean, I'm already like, God this is, I haven't even met this girl, you know, but I give this woman thirty euros and she tells me to relax and take a shower and Jeanette will be in in ten minutes.

So I'm there in this room. And I can hear people in the house, talking or moving around or whatever, and it's a bit, you know . . . but I was hoping that whatever was going to happen was going to give me some relief, you know? Not a sexual thing, I don't . . . (*Unsaid: 'think'*.) Just some . . . I mean, I know it sounds . . . 'Oh that's what everybody says . . . ' but you know . . .

IAN. No, I know.

JOHN. So I just, fuck it, I took a shower in there . . . in the corner. And I dried myself and . . . then I put my clothes back on!

They smile briefly.

And I'm in there maybe fifteen minutes and nothing is happening, you know, so I stick my head out the door, but I don't see anyone, and I decide to wait. And the doorbell goes and I hear the woman bringing in some other guy and she takes him off somewhere. And by this stage . . . I'm like . . . this is just freaking me out, really, but at the same time, like I say, I'm hoping for some . . . you know, I'm hanging in there. So I wait and I hear a bit of movement, and I hear someone leaving so I think maybe it's going to happen now, but then twenty minutes go by so I just, I'm like, forget it.

So I put on my coat and I open the door to go and the woman who let me in is coming down the hall going like,

(*Strong Dublin accent.*) 'What are you doing? Go in and have a shower!' and she comes right up to me and the smell of drink off her, you know? And I'm like, 'Look I'm going to leave it.'

And then this guy appears, you know? Like a total skanger. Just with these really dead eyes, you know? And he's like, 'What's going on?' And they're much louder than they have to be, if you know what I mean.

And for some reason I . . . just . . . decide. That . . . I'm not gonna take this fucking shit anymore, I've just had enough so although I'm probably definitely on a hiding to nothing I say, 'Give me my thirty euros back . . . ' which of course, is madness, you know? But of course this *is* fucking madness, you know?

So she shouts, 'We don't owe you any money – we provide the amenities and that's what you were charged for. We don't owe you a fucking penny!' And your man is like, 'Come on now, you're either going to have to go in and have a shower or you're going to have to go.' But by this stage I suppose these two people represent everything that's wrong with the world to me and it's like I'm . . . I just refuse to accept this, you know? And I'm . . . *demanding* my money back! I just want to have a transaction where some normal rules apply again, you know? And look where I was trying to fucking achieve that! You know?

They smile.

And then, I just, before I know it, your man just hits me right in the stomach! And I mean, I'm not fit, and I haven't been in a fight since I was maybe ten or something! But that feeling of being completely winded, of not being able to breathe and being completely paralysed – it just . . . I just bent over slowly and I could hear this awful groan coming out and it was me making it – you know – completely out of my control. And I just went down and down until I was on my knees on the floor. And I hear your man going, 'Now you brought that on yourself.' And he was so fucking right, you know?

And then they sat me on the stairs, you know? They were getting a bit worried, because I just could not breathe. She's going like, 'What did you hit him for?' And he's saying to me, 'You'll be alright, you'll be alright . . . ' And I felt fucking grateful! It was so stupid but in a mad way, that's what I wanted! I wanted someone to tell me that things were going to be okay. I mean I was really clinging to the fucking wreckage here now, you know?

He sighs deeply.

And . . . I went home. Still completely able to . . . I went in and Mari had my dinner there on the table, you know, chops and peas and potatoes. And the pain in my stomach was . . . I could barely fucking walk, you know? And, of course she . . . the minute she sees me she just . . . she was like 'Oh my God, John, what's happened? Are you alright?'

And I . . . (*He almost starts crying but keeps it together.*) . . . I just turned on her, Ian, you know? I just . . . exploded. And I ate the head off her. I was like an animal. And it was just so . . . sudden. She looked so frightened, I had never seen that look, of real fear, and I was doing it! You know?

He starts crying.

And, I pushed her up against the wall and I told her, 'You're fucking killing me.'

And I . . . grabbed her by the shoulders and I shook her. I shook her so hard. I could feel how small and helpless she was. It was a terrible feeling. And I said to her, 'Don't fucking speak to me anymore. Don't you dare fucking speak to me.' And she just cowered down on the floor – nothing like this had ever happened between us before, you know? And she curled herself up into a little ball there down beside the bin. And the sobs just came out of her, you know? Just the total . . . bewilderment, you know?

Pause. JOHN *is in the deep pit of his self-loathing.*

And after that, like from then on, I couldn't . . . And I just don't understand. How, why I just couldn't have talked to her? She only wanted to help me. But it was like . . . (*Short pause.*) I was in a kind of a storm, you know? You're only just barely hanging on, just hanging in there. And I was frightened that she'd, or anyone would . . . see how weak I was. And how . . . disgusting I was. And she'd hate me, you know? Everything just developed into a kind of paralysis. That's the only way I can describe it. You just can't fucking move, you know?

Because, I think I killed her that day, you know? I mean, I didn't kill her. But I might as well have.

I mean, I don't even know where she was going the night that . . . or where she had been. We didn't even speak to each other before she died, she was on her own, you know? I just feel like I just fucking left her alone in the world, you know? If I could have even slept in the bed beside her, maybe that might have even been enough! You know, I . . . I probably didn't even have to say anything . . . And now I can't go back!

Long pause.

I just . . . I believe in a way that I probably did it to her, Ian, you know?

IAN. No.

JOHN. And that's probably why I've seen her, you know?

IAN. No. I don't . . .

JOHN. Like she only wanted to fucking help me, you know?

IAN. But it was an accident. She was in an accident.

JOHN. But I . . . I mean I think about it. Where would she have been going? She wouldn't have been out on her own in town if . . . you know . . . And she was so kind, you know? I . . . I mean, is it . . . ? Is it that, in some way, she . . . Is she trying to . . .

IAN. I really don't think that . . .

JOHN. Is she trying to hurt me? Or I mean . . .

IAN. Well you see I'm not convinced that . . .

JOHN. Or maybe I've got it wrong. You know? Maybe I've got the whole thing arseways.

Pause.

Maybe she's . . . Maybe she's just trying to save me, you know?

Lights down.

Scene Four

A church bell strikes twice in the distance. It is night. The office is in darkness except for what light spills in from the street. We hear someone coming up the stairs. The door opens and IAN comes in and switches on a lamp or two. LAURENCE comes in and hovers near the door. He is skinny and wears sports gear and runners. It is hard to tell if he is thirty and looks much younger or twenty and looks much older. He has a nervous, twitchy energy and seems like he lives from minute to minute. He has a dirty bandage on his right hand.

IAN. Come in. Come in. It's okay. There's no one else. There's no one in the whole building. This is . . . where I work.

LAURENCE shuts the door. They stand there, IAN doesn't seem to know what to do.

Let me eh . . . I think I have eh . . . would you . . . drink a glass of wine?

LAURENCE (*shrugs*). . . . Yeah.

IAN. Okay . . . Let me, eh . . . Let me . . .

He bustles about and finds the bottle NEASA brought in Scene Two. He finds two mugs.

I say 'glass . . . ' but . . . I'll just . . . Eh . . .

He motions to LAURENCE that he wants to get past him and he goes into the little toilet to wash the mugs. We hear him in there while LAURENCE stands alone in the room. He comes back out with the mugs and stops abruptly.

Corkscrew. Didn't think of that. Didn't think of it. Em.

LAURENCE. You can push it in.

IAN. The . . .

LAURENCE. You can push the cork down. If you have something to . . .

IAN. Like eh . . .

LAURENCE. Just a knife.

IAN. I have a knife. (*He goes to a box which has a few kitchen things.*) Just a cutlery knife . . .

LAURENCE. Yeah, just anything . . .

IAN holds up an ordinary 'knife and fork' knife.

Yeah, you . . .

He goes to IAN who takes the bottle up and they awkwardly jockey for position.

IAN. Will I . . . or . . .

He hands the bottle to LAURENCE.

LAURENCE. Yeah, you just . . . you push it down. My . . . (*He gestures with his bandaged hand.*)

IAN. Oh yes, you just . . .

He takes the bottle and attempts to push the cork in.

LAURENCE. If you, just . . . if you take that, tear off the . . .

IAN. Oh yeah, yeah. (*He uses the knife to cut the seal away from around the cork.*) Actually I'm going to put it on the . . . Just . . .

He puts the bottle on the floor and pushes the cork down with the knife.

It's going down.

LAURENCE (*indicates toilet*). Is that the jacks?

IAN. Oh yeah, go ahead.

LAURENCE goes into the toilet. IAN struggles on the floor. Finally the cork goes in.

(*Calls out.*) I've done it, it's gone in!

He pours two mugs of wine. He stands there, waiting. He seems disconnected for a moment, almost not part of his

own life. The toilet flushes. LAURENCE *emerges.* IAN
hands him a drink.

Now. God, the things we do, ha? Well, cheers.

They drink.

God, it's alright. Here. (*He gives* LAURENCE *another
drink.*) Is your hand alright?

LAURENCE. Ah yeah. It's wrecked.

IAN. What happened to it?

LAURENCE. Ah, a banger. I was eh . . . I was letting off a
banger, with my son, on Hallowe'en. Sometimes my eyes
aren't that good. And the fucking thing nearly blew my
fucking hand off.

IAN. Oh my God. Is it alright?

LAURENCE. Ah it's wrecked. I can only move these two
fingers.

IAN. Oh no.

LAURENCE. Yeah, it's a fucking killer, you know? I can't
work, you know?

IAN. Oh no. What, what do you, what, what are you working
at or . . .

LAURENCE. Ah, I was lined up to get a job driving a van,
but . . .

IAN. Oh no.

LAURENCE. Yeah.

Pause.

IAN. Is it . . . is it healing or are you getting treatment for
it or . . .

LAURENCE. Ah, I'm supposed to keep . . . to go in for
physiotherapy but, it's, it's tricky 'cause I'm trying to keep
a few things organised at the moment and I, sometimes . . .
the appointments don't suit me, then, you know?

IAN. Right . . .

LAURENCE. Because of the times. But this fucking thing is filthy, I need to . . . but they keep you waiting for so long in there, though, you know?

IAN. God, well . . . God, well you . . . you don't want to let it get infected.

LAURENCE. I know. I know. But, yeah, you know, I have to do it. You know?

Pause.

IAN. Are you cold? Do you want me to turn that, turn that on?

LAURENCE. Yeah, I'm freezing. Are you not cold?

IAN. Oh sure, I'll . . . (*He goes and turns on an electric heater.*) This heats up real fast.

Pause.

I'd say it gets pretty cold when you're . . . up there just . . .

LAURENCE. Yeah, it's . . . you know . . . but sometimes you just fucking have to, 'cause . . .

IAN. Yeah . . . Yeah . . . (*Pause.*) I've never eh . . . I've never gone up there, before, you know? I've never . . . this is the . . . I mean . . . Do you, do . . . I, do you, do I pay you now, or do I . . . ?

LAURENCE. Yeah, well, whatever. If you want to get it out of the way, you don't have to think about it then, anymore, you know?

IAN. Yeah, yeah, that's . . . okay, let's . . . okay. (*He counts out some money from his pocket.*) Em. (*He hands it to* LAURENCE.) That's . . .

LAURENCE. Yeah. You don't have to be so nervous.

IAN. Yeah. I know. I'm sorry. I just, em . . . I've never . . .

LAURENCE. Because you're making me nervous.

IAN. Oh no, I don't want to, I'm sorry.

LAURENCE. Yeah, no, it's just, I get, like I just . . .

IAN. I know, I know, it's contagious. I know. I've never . . .

LAURENCE indicates sound system.

LAURENCE. Do you want to turn on some music or something?

IAN. Yeah! Yeah, I'll . . .

IAN goes over to the stereo and starts looking through some CDs.

God, what'll I put on?

LAURENCE. Just whatever you want.

IAN. Yeah, but em . . . Do you like the Eagles?

LAURENCE. Don't know them.

IAN. No. Hold on, someone burned this for me . . .

He puts on a CD. It is slow, mellow country rock.

This is, you know, it's quite laid back.

LAURENCE makes a slight move as though he may be coming towards IAN. IAN halts him with his voice.

You have a son?

LAURENCE. Yeah.

IAN. Is he . . . How old is he?

LAURENCE (*without much enthusiasm*). He's six.

IAN. Wow, is he . . .

LAURENCE. He's with his ma. She's nuts, you know, her mother looks after him more.

IAN. Right.

LAURENCE. Yeah, but look, I don't really wanna . . .

IAN. Yeah, of course, I'm sorry.

Pause.

Are you a bit warmer?

LAURENCE. Yeah, yeah.

IAN. God . . . I'd say it's cold up there, though, when you're waiting around, is it?

LAURENCE. Yeah it's weird, you know? I mean, it's a bit . . .

IAN. Mmm.

LAURENCE. Yeah, I got the shit kicked out of me one time up there, you know?

IAN. Oh no . . .

LAURENCE. Yeah, ah it was my own fault. I wouldn't even be out there tonight only, I've been staying with my cousin in this flat in town. But this young one came to stay there, and she said there was some money gone out of her bag, and . . . it wasn't me, like, but . . . now . . . I have to try to . . .

IAN. Yeah . . .

LAURENCE. Get a few quid together.

IAN. I know.

LAURENCE. So I can go back and . . .

IAN. Yeah . . .

LAURENCE. I don't even want to go back, though, but I need an address.

IAN. Yeah.

LAURENCE. This is where you work, yeah?

IAN. Yeah, well, yeah . . . I've been here for a few months, you know?

LAURENCE. What do you work at?

IAN. Well, I'm a therapist, you know?

LAURENCE. A therapist?

IAN. Yeah, you know . . .

LAURENCE. What, do you . . .

IAN. Well, you know, people can come, and . . . talk to me, or . . .

LAURENCE. What, like mad people?

IAN. No, not mad . . . Just maybe . . . people who might just feel a little bit . . . stuck, you know? And maybe they . . . just need a . . . just another point of view on what's going on, if they're carrying, you know, a big burden, you know? Of some guilt maybe. You know? Or where they might feel it's hard to go on because they've got themselves just in a bit of a corner, because they're worried about other people, or maybe it's just that they have some old feeling . . . Maybe even from years ago, just even sometimes things can happen to us when we're children, and that, you know, maybe that sets the tone for how people get on later. Where maybe they get a bit stuck. And maybe I can just invite them to consider something that maybe they didn't think was that important before, but, you know, maybe it was . . . and . . .

LAURENCE. Do you ever hypnotise people?

IAN. No, no I don't. We . . . no, it's, it's all fully conscious. It's . . . about perceiving reality, I suppose.

Pause. LAURENCE *puts his drink down as if to move towards* IAN.

I have a daughter. That I haven't seen . . . either . . . you know, much . . . She's with her mother . . . I mean, I know what you . . . when you say . . .

LAURENCE *moves towards* IAN. IAN *stands very still.* LAURENCE *puts his hand on* IAN's *arm and gently moves him closer.*

LAURENCE. It's alright. Don't be frightened.

LAURENCE *takes* IAN's *drink and puts it down.* IAN *is shaking.* LAURENCE *pulls* IAN *towards him and holds him, swaying to the music.* IAN *tentatively puts his arms around* LAURENCE. *Suddenly the music breaks into faster, wholly inappropriate hillbilly fiddle/banjo music.*

IAN. Sorry!

He goes to the stereo and turns it off.

God, that's look, em . . . when I say that I haven't, you
know, done this, or gone up to the park before, I don't mean
that I haven't just gone up to the park at night, you know . . .
I mean. (*Pause.*) I mean I've never been with a man.
(*Pause.*) Do you understand me?

LAURENCE (*shrugs*). That's alright. The men who go up
there are all fucking married, you know? Loads of them are!
That's why . . . they . . . (*Pause.*) What difference does it
make? (*Pause.*) You should just do what you want to do,
you know? (*Pause.*) Put on the other music. Put on the
music that was on before. (*Reassuringly.*) I have nowhere
else to go.

*IAN goes to the machine and puts on the other music again.
He goes to the bottle and pours them both another drink.
He hands a mug to* LAURENCE, *avoiding eye contact.*
LAURENCE *takes his hand.* IAN *looks into* LAURENCE*'s
eyes.* LAURENCE *returns his gaze, and then places* IAN*'s
hand against his crotch, holding it there.* IAN *starts to
caress* LAURENCE*'s crotch and they move closer together.*

Lights down.

Scene Five

It is daytime. Bright sunlight streams into the room. As the scene progresses, the room should become more dusky. There are dust sheets on the desk and most of the furniture and books are gone. There are boxes all around the office, and IAN *is there packing books, files, etc away. There is a little transistor radio on the floor and indistinct daytime radio is playing while* IAN *packs. The intercom buzzer goes off and* IAN *goes to answer it, maybe a bit pissed off, he doesn't expect anyone.*

IAN. Yeah? Hello? Hello? Yeah, hold on. (*He presses the buzzer to release the door.*) Hello? Are you in? Hello? What? Hello? (*He presses the button again.*) Hello? Are you there? What? (*There is a knock at his door,* IAN *opens it to reveal* JOHN, *carrying a present.*)

Oh, hello!

JOHN. Sorry, I'm barging in on you.

IAN. No! No! I just I couldn't hear . . . come in, come in!

JOHN (*coming in*). No, I just . . . I've had this, fucking . . . I've had it in the car and I, 'cause I wanted to get you something.

IAN. Oh no!

JOHN. And then, of course, I've been driving around with it in the boot for the last six weeks, you know what I mean?

IAN. Oh no . . .

JOHN. It's nothing.

IAN. Oh no . . .

JOHN. It's a lamp, it's nothing.

IAN. Oh but still, thanks, you . . . come in, sit down, there's nowhere to sit.

JOHN. And I was going by, and I thought . . . God, I should just call in, and I thought, well, it's lunchtime, he probably won't have anyone there, and . . .

IAN. No, no, I'm . . .

JOHN. Janey Mack, you're . . .

IAN. Well, no, it's lucky you . . . I'm moving! I'm going, you know?

JOHN. You're moving your office?

IAN. I'm, well, no, I'm moving. I'm, I'm going down to Limerick, believe it or not.

JOHN. Limerick?

IAN. Yeah, my fiancé is there and . . . (*As though these are tedious little details that are too boring to go into.*) with our . . . baby, and some . . . friends of hers have lent her a house there, so . . .

JOHN. Yeah.

IAN. I'm going down . . . and I've, you know, I'm applying for a . . . I've an interview down there. For a post so . . .

JOHN. Yeah.

IAN (*doesn't understand* JOHN'S *reference*). Mm. You know, so . . . it's time, and . . .

JOHN. Yeah, well great! That sounds good. Dublin's . . . you know . . .

IAN. Yeah.

JOHN. It's a tough town.

Pause.

IAN. Yeah, well, look, let me, move some of this stuff. Sit down!

IAN *bustles around.*

JOHN. Ah, I'm not gonna stay, really.

IAN. No, no! Look, the kettle is still . . . on the go, we're
   still . . . Let me . . .

   IAN *disappears into the toilet with the kettle.*

   (*Off.*) So, how are you keeping?

JOHN. Yeah. You know, I'm good! You know, I have to say,
   I'm good. Thank God, you know? I'm getting there, you
   know, definitely, and I really, you know . . .

   IAN *re-emerges and plugs the kettle in.*

   I just wanted to say thanks, because, you know . . .

IAN. No, no. You did the work, you know?

JOHN. Yeah, no, but, you know, I mean . . . I wanted to, you
   know . . .

IAN. God, well, you didn't have to. And you shouldn't have.
   Really, you know?

JOHN. Yeah, well . . .

IAN. No, well, thank you, I mean . . . will I open it?

JOHN. Yeah, yeah! Go ahead, open it, it's nothing, you know?
   It's really, it's not . . .

   IAN *opens the paper.*

   I mean, I have no eye for these things. The girl in the shop,
   you know, I – it was her really. I mean, I said it was a
   present and she said, who is it for, and then of course I
   realised, 'God, I know nothing about this man!' You know?
   (*They laugh.*) Because I don't! I mean, it's weird, isn't it?

IAN. Well, it's, you know, it's . . . (*Unsaid: 'normal'.*)

JOHN. So I said, it was just a thank-you present really.

IAN. Tch, God, no . . .

JOHN. And she . . .

   IAN *produces a stunning antique lamp from the box.*

IAN. Oh my God!

JOHN. Ah, no, sure . . .

IAN. This is too much.

JOHN. No, it's nothing.

IAN. Is it, it's . . . an antique, or . . . ?

JOHN. It's, ah, it's from the thirties or fucking something, I don't know.

IAN. No, well that's, it's too much . . .

JOHN. Please, no. Do you like it?

IAN. It's beautiful, really . . .

JOHN. Well, you know, thank you, you know, that's . . . (*Unsaid: 'why I'm here'.*) I . . .

IAN. Thank you, really, thanks, God . . .

JOHN *produces a card in an envelope from his pocket.*

JOHN. And this is just a little card. You know, to go . . .

IAN. Oh, God . . . God, thanks, thanks John, really.

IAN *reads the card.*

JOHN (*interrupting* IAN *reading it*). Ah, read it later.

IAN. Tch. God, no, well. I don't know what to say now.

JOHN. Ah there's . . . (*Unsaid: 'nothing to say'.*)

IAN. God, well let me make you a cup of tea. Here, sit down, take off your coat.

JOHN. I'm grand, really.

IAN *produces an old stool from somewhere.*

IAN. No, sit down there, here.

JOHN *sits a bit awkwardly.*

So, God, how are you keeping?

JOHN. I'm good, you know? I'm good. I'm . . . I've just bought an apartment.

IAN. Oh wow, so we're both . . .

JOHN. We're both moving. Yeah . . . nearly finished the, the legal . . . which can be a nightmare . . . but it's . . . it's . . .

IAN. If it's what you've got to do, that's right, I know . . .

JOHN. Yeah, it's lovely. It's down there on the seafront, just there near St Anne's Park.

IAN. Oh very nice, yeah, I know there.

JOHN. Yeah, it's those ones there . . .

IAN. They're nice, yeah.

JOHN. Yeah, so whole new . . .

  IAN *finds teabags and cups.*

IAN. And you're . . . You're good . . . in yourself, and . . .

JOHN. I'm . . . really good, Ian, you know? I have to say. I'm looking forward to the move. And I've . . . actually been in the house again, this last month, you know?

IAN. Oh right! God, that's . . . do you take sugar?

JOHN. No, no, it's fine.

IAN. Good, because I don't eh . . .

  They laugh a little.

JOHN. No I don't, anyway, so . . . and eh, yeah, I've been there, in the house. And I mean, there was a time, as you know, I couldn't even have envisaged myself spending even one night there, so, no I'm . . .

IAN. But you're going to move on and . . .

JOHN. I'm moving on . . . It's, it's just . . . It just feels right. It just feels like that's, that's what . . . I . . . what I . . . that's just what I want to do! I mean, I don't want to be some old guy on his own in there. You know? That house is all to do with me and Mari, and it's even too big for two people – it was too big when we moved in. I mean, if there had been kids, okay, but, you know, that didn't happen and . . . I mean, I just feel like my life isn't over, you know? Like why should I stay in the house out of some kind of mad fucking duty to fucking . . . you know . . . I mean . . .

IAN. I know, you're right, I know. I mean it's so . . .

JOHN. I mean we create these fucking . . .

IAN. I know, I know . . .

JOHN. These mad . . .

IAN. I know. I know. But that's, you know, that's great, you're . . .

JOHN. Yeah . . . I'm . . . you know, I'm getting on with it, and I really see it now like a . . . like a new chapter is opening up, and like *you* know, there was a time I could never have thought that that was even possible! You know, I mean . . .

IAN. Well, that's great, I mean, that's . . .

JOHN. And that's why, I mean, I want to thank you really, because . . .

IAN. Yeah, well, like I say, you did the work.

JOHN. . . . I don't know what I . . . would've . . .

IAN. Well, look I'm . . . I'm glad. I'm happy for you, I mean that. And, you know, I hope, you know, you . . .

JOHN. My fucking brother introduced me to a woman, there, you know?

IAN. Oh . . . ?

JOHN. Yeah, I mean, he's a prick. He can be a bit of an arsehole. But he's, you know . . . he's alright, you know, really.

IAN. Yeah, I know what you mean.

JOHN. Yeah, him and his missus were killed asking me over for some dinner there four or five weeks ago. I was like . . . (*Sarcastic.*) 'Yeah, right . . . ' you know. Because I can sometimes do without that, you know what I mean? But I . . . went over. There were a few people there. This girl was there. I knew her, though, slightly, from before, she used to work where I – she used to work there, coincidentally, and she's . . . she's a bit younger than me now, you know, but . . .

IAN (*shrugs*). Well . . .

JOHN. Yeah, sure, what fucking difference does it make? I agree. Although . . . if she was a good bit *older* than me now, the shoe might well be very much on the other fucking foot now, you know what I mean?

They laugh.

No, but, she's a nice girl, you know? Sure, I'm not . . . we just went to the pictures and had a drink, you know, just . . . (*Short pause.*) We're going to the theatre tomorrow night.

IAN. Oh!

JOHN. I know! (*As though the theatre is rubbish.*) 'Good luck!' Ah, but, sure . . .

IAN. Yeah, well, that's . . . (*Short pause.*) Don't feel that you have to rush into anything, John, you know?

JOHN. No, no, no, no, I'm not, no. I'm, it just feels like it's just a part of . . . just a new . . . it's all just a new . . . it's good, you know? Don't worry.

IAN. Yeah, yeah, no, I'm . . .

JOHN. But Jesus! Do you know who I saw?

IAN. Yeah?

JOHN. Vivien.

IAN. Yeah?

JOHN. Vivien, the . . .

IAN. Yeah.

JOHN. The object of my . . . my downfall. The big . . .

IAN. Yeah.

JOHN. Yeah, saw her there at a do. God, it was weird, you know? I mean she had great sympathy for me and everything, but it was really like nothing had ever happened? Between us? Weird, you know? And do you know what was really weird? I realised we had *nothing* in common. What about that, you know?

IAN *nods.*

Serious. Serious fucking shit. I came away thinking, 'I don't even like this woman', you know? Bizarre. When I . . . (*Short pause.*) Mad.

Pause.

IAN. God, John. Well, you know, it sounds like you're doing really well though, you know?

JOHN. Well, I'm, you know . . .

IAN. But you're getting out, you're meeting people . . . and . . .

JOHN. Ah, I'm just, I'm just taking it handy. And . . . it was a great help, you were a great help, Ian, to me, you know? I mean it and . . . I wish you all the best, you know?

IAN. Well, look, I wish you all the best too, John. I really do, you know, and . . . you know, it makes me feel good to see you . . . that you're, you know . . .

JOHN. Well, thanks. Thank you. You know? (*Short pause.*) And I'll . . . I only came to . . . I better let you . . . .

IAN. Well, I'm, yeah . . . I said I'd drop the keys back this afternoon and . . . I'm . . .

JOHN. Do you want a hand with anything?

IAN. No, no, no . . .

JOHN. Are you sure?

IAN. Really, don't . . . I'm, I'm nearly there now.

They are standing. JOHN *picks up his coat.*

JOHN. Okay.

IAN. So, no ghosts.

JOHN. No. No ghosts. (*He exhales.*) But, I'll tell you, you know, even if I saw one, Ian, it's not . . . I mean, seeing

something is one thing but . . . it's how it makes you *feel*,
isn't it? It's how that makes you feel. That's what's
important. Someone could see something and it doesn't
really matter. Someone else'll see it and . . . it's the end of
the world, you know?

IAN (*affirmative*). Mmm.

JOHN. That's the reality, you know? What it *does* to you is the
reality.

IAN. I know.

JOHN. But you don't believe in ghosts anyway, Ian. You've got
it sussed.

They are moving towards the door.

IAN. John, there was a time I would've given anything to see
one. Just to know that there was . . . something else. Do you
know what I mean?

JOHN. Sure.

IAN. Just something else, besides all the . . . you know . . .
the pain and the confusion. Just something that gave everything . . . *some* meaning, you know? I'm talking about God,
really, you know?

JOHN. I know. Where is he?

IAN. I know. But don't get me wrong. I think you had a real
experience. I think you really experienced something – but
I think it happened because you needed to experience it.

JOHN. Yeah, I know . . .

IAN. You were pulling all this . . . you felt maybe you couldn't
move on without being . . . punished somehow and . . .

JOHN. I know.

IAN. It happened! But . . . I don't believe you saw a ghost.
Does that make sense?

JOHN. Well, yeah, it makes sense to me now, but there was a
time it really wouldn't have, you know? (*Pause.*) But that
was a different time.

IAN. Yeah, it was.

JOHN *opens the door.*

JOHN. I'll tell you, the mind, it's mad isn't it?

IAN. John, we know nothing. We just know nothing really.

JOHN. We're just barely fucking hanging in there, really, aren't we?

IAN. Well, some better than others. But you're doing good, John, you know? Considering, I mean, you know?

JOHN. I know. I know that. But I had to fucking go there to find that out. Do you know what I mean?

IAN. I do. I know.

Pause.

JOHN. Look, I'll love you and leave you. Good luck with everything, alright?

IAN. Well you too, and thanks, for the present. It really is so thoughtful . . .

JOHN (*interrupting*). Ah, it's nothing, good luck.

They shake hands.

I'll see you.

IAN. Well . . . Actually, I'll wait here till you get out down there. And I can buzz it if . . . 'cause it's still . . .

JOHN. Oh, nothing changes! I'll see you Ian, good luck.

IAN. I'll see you, John, bye now.

IAN *hovers near the open door while* JOHN *goes down. He picks a flier up off the floor at the threshold and crumples it up. He picks two books off the floor and looks at the back of one of them. We hear the outer door slam shut. In the distance we hear the faint sound of an ice-cream van's music.*

(*Calls out.*) Did you get out?

There is no answer.

IAN *throws one of the two books in a box near the door. He shuts the door and crosses the room to throw the other book in a different box.*

In the darkening gloom of the afternoon, we see that MARI's *ghost has appeared behind the door. She is looking at* IAN, *just as* JOHN *described her; she wears her red coat, which is filthy, her hair is wet. She looks beaten up. She looks terrifying.*

IAN *has his back to her at his desk, going through some old post. But he seems to sense something and turns.*

Lights down.

A Nick Hern Book

Shining City first published in Great Britain as a paperback original in 2004 by Nick Hern Books Limited, 14 Larden Road, London W3 7ST in association with the Royal Court Theatre, London, and the Gate Theatre, Dublin.

Shining City copyright © 2004 Conor McPherson

Conor McPherson has asserted his right to be identified as the author of this work

Cover Image: Conor McPherson

Typeset by Country Setting, Kingsdown, Kent CT14 8ES
Printed and bound in Great Britain by Bookmarque, Croydon, Surrey

A CIP catalogue record for this book is available from the British Library

ISBN 1 85459 819 8